The Diversity Dashboard

'The Diversity Dashboard will delight managers who want precise, accessible advice on handling cross-cultural differences in today's frenetic business world. Do not be fooled by the graphics and easy style; The Diversity Dashboard is a rich and invaluable resource.'

Fons Trompenaars, author of *Riding the Waves of Culture*

'If you are flying fast, The Diversity Dashboard offers some quick and effective navigation through many of the cultural differences you are likely to traverse – a great way to start your journey into the intricacies of intercultural communication.'

Milton Bennett, Ph.D., author of *Basic Concepts of Intercultural Communication*

'The Diversity Dashboard is a breath of fresh air. It turns a complex topic into an accessible format and easy-to-use tool. The anecdotes and case studies are presented in plain and simple English, making them immediately applicable in today's busy life.'

Richard D. Lewis, author of *When Cultures Collide*

'Recognising cultural change provides competitive edge … it's a challenge, but it's one that I think can be overcome. That's where The Diversity Dashboard is useful. It is a quick reference guide – a great travelling companion – which can help you gain the determination and enthusiasm to reach out to fresh areas and to do so with vigour, commitment and confidence.'

Sir Roger Carr, Chairman Centrica PLC and President CBI

'Will it fly? Nope, you have to fly it. The Diversity Dashboard is a lightweight manual, a basic checklist for piloting projects and organizations through cultural turbulence.'

Dr George Simons, creator of diversophy®

The
Diversity
Dashboard

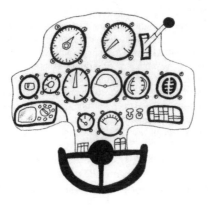

A manager's guide to navigating in cross-cultural turbulence

Dr Deborah Swallow and Eilidh Milnes

First published in 2013 by
Infinite Ideas Limited
36 St Giles
Oxford
OX1 3LD
United Kingdom
www.infideas.com

A CIP catalogue record for this book is available from the British Library

ISBN 978-1-908984-19-7

Cover designed by Cylinder
Illustrations by Mark Edmonds
Printed by Bell & Bain Ltd., Glasgow

The format of *The Diversity Dashboard* has been inspired by *Resonate* by Nancy Duarte, who kindly gifted the paper people graphics used on pages 20 and 21. Visit www.duarte.com.

If something surprises you, annoys you or you find it completely ridiculous, you may be in the presence of a cultural difference.

John Mole

This book uses the very latest augmented reality on the cover. Just follow these three easy steps on your smartphone or tablet and see the book come to life:

1. **Visit the App Store on your iPhone or iPad, or the Play Store on your Android device, and download the free arpeople app.**

2. **Activate the app.**

3. **Use it to scan the cover – to hold the visuals on your device double tap the screen.**

Enjoy the little pilot animation. Do let us know what you think of this new technology. Thank you.

Contents

Introduction

Language is what we hear. Culture is how we understand.

Dr Deborah Swallow

The global business environment demands a new skill set and the willingness to push ourselves into uncomfortable and uncertain situations. It has also created a group of businesspeople who are willing to seek out new experiences in new international contexts and who gain a competitive career advantage over their stay-at-home colleagues.

These people are no longer just expats assigned to one country but real global managers: leading global teams within multinational organizations, launching innovative global products, managing supply chains and processes worldwide, all together with juggling more traditional managerial roles at base. Whatever and wherever they do it, they need to be able to switch their approach rapidly between different peoples and different cultures, and live with multiple world views.

We used to experience culture shock ('Oh, did they really do/say that?') when we travelled between countries. Now we experience culture shock just sitting at our desks as we engage with people in the workplace who come from all around the world. Trouble is, if we don't understand the context behind what has been said, it is all too easy to take offence. If we don't understand how to manage people from diverse backgrounds, productivity suffers and relationships deteriorate. Life being what it is, not all people communicate in the same way. However, just like you, everyone wants to be treated with understanding and respect.

The most ordinary thing in the world is to see things through your own eyes. The most extraordinary thing is to see things through the eyes of others.

Eilidh Milnes

The Diversity Dashboard: a manager's guide to navigating in cross-cultural turbulence will improve your understanding of how different people think, work and feel. It will help you break down cultural barriers and guide you to a more effective, cooperative and harmonious workplace. This book is aimed at those who work in global corporations where English is the primary language, where staff are multicultural, and who are either at head office or connected virtually across the world. Based on more than twenty years' experience, as authors we wanted to turn this complex topic into simple insights, and turn true-life case studies into short 'culture crashes'. Uniquely, we'll give both sides of the story and turn each incident into a 'culture tip'.

Reading this book will help you to:

1. Gain insight into the lives of others in similar situations – how they think, feel and behave,

2. Acquire essential knowledge to help you feel more confident when dealing with people from different countries,

3. Learn how to overcome problems and challenges arising from cultural diversity,

4. Handle awkward colleagues and clients – giving tips and techniques for cultural awareness,

and most importantly,

5. Think differently: give you the understanding to make sense of cultural experiences – past, present and future.

The difference between this and other cross-cultural awareness books is its simplicity. This new book contains the essential theory and research which underpins cross-cultural communication in an easy to grasp and jargon-busting way. It is a quick reference guide for people in a hurry, on the move or, as we like to say, 'flying from their desks'.

As a manual to apply to everyday conflict issues and cultural misunderstandings, *The Diversity Dashboard* will enlighten and entertain. It will help you become more tolerant and less judgemental – in fact, become more creative. That's because solving cross-cultural issues requires imagination, reconciliation and optimization, not compromise.

Successful international managers reconcile dilemmas daily and see cross-cultural differences as an opportunity to get the best of both worlds. This means creating new ways of looking at and dealing with our differences. Not fighting each other about how we are, or are not, going to behave, but combining our strengths and avoiding compromise because that often leads to mediocre solutions.

Whether you are flying from your desk or from a train, boat or plane, *The Diversity Dashboard* will help you be more confident, interculturally competent and competitive in this rapidly changing globalized world.

Background: a note from the authors

Culture is a kind of unchained dark force undermining internationally operating firms at every turn.

Nigel Holden

Why this topic?

Unfortunately, most English-speaking nations have little concept of cross-cultural differences. The world speaks English and big business is constructed in our own image. We do, we act and we think business

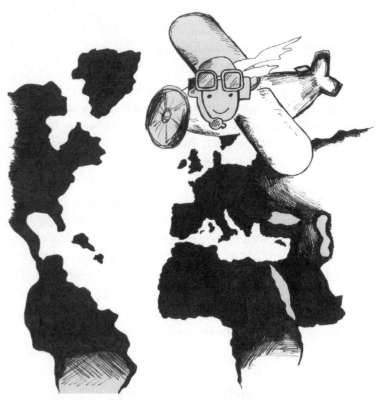

in our cultural mode, and expect the world to do the same. Therefore, when things go wrong – and they repeatedly do – we tend to throw business solutions at these business problems and never solve the real issue.

When confronted with cross-cultural differences, organizations expect their middle managers to miraculously obtain instant multicultural management skills. Everything is reduced to an operational management issue. The result is that cross-cultural differences and issues are managed, even marginalized, without ever building more trust between ourselves.

Compounding the problem, most firms consider diversity and inclusion as being more of a compliance issue than a sound strategy for developing business growth. When competition for both talent and customers is so fierce, taking a compliance-issue approach will seriously inhibit your competitive edge at home and abroad. Helping your people develop cultural intelligence will reap dividends: building on brand reputation, increasing customer and staff retention and adding to your bottom line.

Companies can no longer assume that all the smart people in the world are born within a twenty-mile radius of their headquarters...

Christopher A. Bartlett

Why now?

Until recently, globalization for businesses generally meant taking the ways of the West to the East. Eastern leaders were invited to learn Western leadership principles at our business schools. But things have changed. The reverse is happening. Now, Chinese and Indian companies are introducing new business philosophies on how to manage to the West, adding to the influence already exercised by the Japanese.

Also, corporates are recruiting from a much larger pool of diverse people with culturally different backgrounds. You will easily find, in any financial firm in the City of London, employees who come from Bulgaria, Bangalore and Brazil. No longer do employees only suffer from culture shock as they travel to a new host country, but they experience, along with their organizations, daily multicultural shocks from the numerous different employees that come and work for them.

Why cultural intelligence?

We are all internationalists now. We are dealing with foreigners in our own community, travelling abroad more, dealing at a distance with people from other places through outsourcing or email, phone and videoconferencing. For a long time it has been assumed that with everyone using English as a lingua franca we can readily understand each other. This isn't true. And performance at work suffers. Those who dismiss cultural differences as insignificant because 'we all know our objectives, goals and deadlines' miss the fact that these have been fashioned in our own North American and Northern European image.

We need to develop the mindset and techniques to adapt our ways to learn about, understand and appreciate the values, ways of doing things and unique qualities of other cultures. It's time to develop the intercultural skills that will serve us through our adult working life. This covers how we create cultural awareness, what qualities we need to deal successfully with other cultures, and how to operate successfully within the 'rules' of people from other cultures. Not only is this cultural intelligence a business skill for adults, but it is also a life skill for our families.

But it has advantages for organizations too!

Confidence plus cultural awareness with cultural intelligence makes for a serious competitive advantage.

- 97 per cent of British bosses think they should make a greater effort to learn about the business etiquette of other cultures.

- 96 per cent rely on the fact that most people in business can speak English.

- 62 per cent admit they find themselves 'playing it by ear' and taking the lead from those they are meeting or travelling with when they are abroad on business.

Why you need this book

Leaders at all levels need to be able to deal effectively with the cultural differences that can hinder successful working relationships and promote those that enhance business performance. The ability to connect with people and build successful teams in cross-cultural environments is a crucial competency. And building a culturally competent organization should be the focus of all global managers and HR executives.

But how do modern leaders create effective collaboration between people who, sometimes literally, come from different worlds? How do they build trust, instil a sense of belonging and create a sense of relatedness? Actively creating cross-cultural understanding in a company is not just an operational issue; it takes a proactive engagement from leaders at all levels to commit.

Over many years we have worked with leadership teams of different companies and nationalities, and there is a clear distinction between the organizations that enjoy and embrace cultural diversity and those that don't. Between those that see it as a challenge which motivates them, and those that try to avoid it. Between those that experience the tangible benefits it brings and the positive impact it has on business performance, and those that don't ... yet.

What we do know is those organizations that align their people and their culture by creating a sense of relatedness and belonging, team spirit and mutual trust, outperform those that don't. And that takes cultural intelligence. So, take to the skies with us and let the 'Little Pilot' start you on a journey of discovery about the world of cultural differences in the workplace so you can become more culturally sensitive. Throughout, you'll find helpful quotes from colleagues and clients.

Enjoy flying from your desk!
Debby Swallow and Eilidh Milnes

How to get the most out of this book

Use this book as a workbook

Use The Diversity Dashboard for your notes and ideas. It will chart your progress. At a glance you will be able to see how well you have reflected on the differences that make a difference in your global working environment. After introducing a Diversity Instrument, each chapter finishes with a Cultural Confidence form for you to jot down your own insights and possible action steps to apply the success strategies that are relevant to you. As you read, if an idea has resonance with you, stop and say to yourself: How can I apply that insight to my working life? Will that suggestion work for me? How can I use that to build a cultural bridge for my team? Perhaps it has more relevance to your colleagues, if so share it at your next meeting.

Use the illustrations as anchors

Throughout this book we've used a number of icons to signpost different kinds of information, anecdotes and activities. This is to make it easy for you to 'dip in and out' of the book during your cultural journey. Here's what they mean:

Culture crash

Sometimes known as a critical incident, it is a short story of an event where behaviour and/ or outcome have been very different from expected. It need not be dramatic, but it demonstrates differences in cultural beliefs, values, attitudes or behaviour.

Culture tip

This provides an explanation of why the culture crash has taken place and involves the identification of behaviour deemed to have been particularly helpful or unhelpful in a given situation. Together with the culture crash, it should make you stop and think. Take a moment to diagnose what happened and learn from it. In the context of your work, raise questions about how this might apply to your own situation.

Cultural insight

This gives a deeper understanding or helpful insight into a particular aspect of culture.

Story

This is an anecdote that we thought interesting and is self-explanatory.

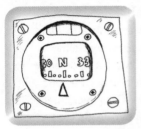

Cultural competence check

This is a little question and answer activity to help you explore what you are learning. Many are taken from the Cultural Competence Diversophy Card Deck and are used with permission of Dr George Simons: www.diversophy.com

Cultural compass

Helpful how-to lists or strategies for successful intercultural interaction.

Confidence booster

This is a tip to help you develop confidence in your foreign exchanges; it may contain advice, an activity or it may be something to guide your thinking – but it will enhance your cultural intelligence.

Visit **www.thediversitydashboard.com/freezone** to download a range or resources and support materials.

1 The cultural cockpit

Greetings. I am pleased to see we are different. May we together become greater than the sum of both of us.

Vulcan greeting from *Star Trek*

Taking time to understand how others think, feel and behave helps to create a more harmonious workplace, increases productivity and empowers global teams. We all do things differently because we have different cultural backgrounds, backgrounds that give us the feeling of 'how we do things around here' and 'how we think of ourselves'. We learn these rules as children and often they are so deeply embedded that we don't even question them.

So what does that mean?

As an example, people from the English-speaking world and north-west European societies are very individualistic. It's normal for them to talk about 'using initiative' and 'being empowered', but someone who comes from a group-oriented culture, like Japan, won't understand those concepts in the same way and will respond differently. A smiling Jamaican might easily misinterpret the soft laughter or shy smile of an Asian; Jamaicans smile readily and easily while Asians do so when they are uncomfortable or embarrassed. Behaviour is relative to context.

People are people the world over with different perspectives and views. The cultural trick is to develop the ability to blend beliefs.

Eilidh Milnes

Enlightenment comes when you see things differently. There is an old adage: do unto others as they do unto you. This may seem sage advice – however, it does make the assumption that there is an underlying similarity and general understanding. Standing by the coffee machine recently, we overheard this comment: 'I cannot understand his attitude. I treated him just the way I would like to be treated...' 'Mmm,' we thought, 'you could try treating him the way *he* wants to be treated.'

Better communication skills don't solve this problem. Understandably, you see the world through your own eyes and behave accordingly. To create better rapport, first you have to understand what lenses you are using and how they influence the way you see the world – rather like looking through a pair of spectacles. Next, you need to see how the world looks through other people's spectacles. Then you need to develop the attitude, skills and behaviour to adapt your communication to build bridges of intercultural understanding. Ultimately, this is what cultural intelligence (or intercultural competence) is all about: awareness, knowledge, attitude and skills.

Because, without this intercultural understanding, the 'MIS' Factor is at play: MISperception leading to MISinterpretation, causing

MISevaluation that creates MIStrust. Which doesn't engender a happy workplace. (See Chapter 20 Cross-cultural competence)

The cockpit metaphor

Imagine going on a journey and boarding an aeroplane. You are the pilot. You take your seat in the cockpit and systematically check all of the instruments before you take off. You've logged your flight plan with air traffic control, you know your destination. Now you need to check the weather forecast during your journey and that you have enough fuel on board. You'll do a few calculations to establish what bearing you need to take, how long the journey will last and make any adjustments to ensure you arrive at the right place, at the right time and with passengers in the right frame of mind, thanks to your preparation and planning.

You can do the same checks when working across cultures.

The cultural cockpit is a device to help you navigate across a culturally diverse workforce. It helps you to take your bearings (understand yourself), guides you in how to adjust your heading (assess the culture you will be working with), and set your speed (the pace at which you can do business). In fact, the cultural cockpit has all the instruments and tools you need to safely travel across the globe, address any turbulence and have a safe landing in a multicultural work environment.

The book cannot possibly cover 101 ways to work in 101 different cultures, but what it can do is guide your thinking and help you adjust your flaps in order to have a turbulence-free flight. The main feature in the cultural cockpit is the Diversity Dashboard which has fifteen instruments to check against to calibrate your flight path (your journey of discovery). Once you have assessed these and logged them into your internal flight management system (your modus operandi) you will be good to go! Like first learning to drive, once you have identified what to do and made the first somewhat self-conscious and awkward initial attempts, confidence and competence quickly come with practice.

But there is one important factor to take into account before you can take off. You need to get your wings. You need a triple A rating to operate your plane. Facts about another culture are not sufficient for you to fly. You need to understand yourself and your own culture first. Then you need to be able to compare and contrast other cultures with your own (have the tools and techniques) to understand the gap. Finally, you have to have the right attitude and willingness to be flexible in your approach.

Getting your wings: the triple 'A' rating in cultural intelligence

These are the three As you need to attain your wings and become culturally competent:

- **Awareness of your own culture**: knowledge about yourself and your core values and how these are expressed in attitudes, behaviours and communication in the workplace.

- **Assessment of other cultures**: awareness of others and the ability to compare and contrast otherness with various tools and techniques.

- **Action**: continuing curiosity to learn more, the willingness to adapt and be flexible, and the ability to identify and respond creatively to cultural challenges and conflicts in ways that both respect and engage the other person.

Confidence booster

Cultural competency is not a state of achievement; it's a process of learning how to learn about other cultures.

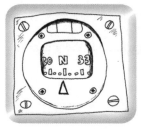

Cultural competence check

The shortest road to cultural intelligence is knowledge of other cultures.

   True or false?

Answer: False

Yes, knowledge is needed, but the culturally intelligent person has developed both the skills and attitudes required to interact successfully with people of different cultures – an essential competence in today's multicultural societies.

2 Your flight plan

It is good to have an end to journey toward; but it is the journey that matters, in the end.

Ernest Hemingway

Before you step into the cockpit you need to file a flight plan, heading for intercultural competence. Air traffic control may think it's a long way off, but you can tell them the journey will take you through six stages.* Others have done it before you. It's a safe route.

Your journey towards intercultural competence

Intercultural competence isn't a destination; it isn't something you suddenly achieve – it's a journey. It's a journey of six stages, and we know that because people make sense of cultural differences in predictable ways as they learn to become more competent intercultural communicators. Basically, we journey from a point where we believe our own culture is central to reality to a point where our own culture is seen within an expanded notion of world views. You can compare it to growing up: at two you think the world revolves around you; by the time you are married and your children are teenagers you see life from a very different perspective.

* Developmental model of intercultural sensitivity: Milton Bennett (1994) www.idrinstitute.org

Let the journey begin...

Stage 1: Denial

Individuals experience their own culture as the only 'real' one, either because of their own isolation, because differences aren't noticed or because of wilful ignorance.

Stage 2: Defence

We know about others but our way is the most 'evolved' or the best way to live: an us-versus-them mentality in which existing assumptions are reinforced and any comment directed toward our own culture is perceived as an attack. Negative stereotyping can take place.

Stage 3: Minimization

We have come to realize that our similarities outweigh our differences. Individuals tell themselves that people are the same everywhere – a superficially benign attitude. In other words, people who adopt this point of view generally approach intercultural situations with the assurance that a simple awareness of the fundamental patterns of human interaction is sufficient for successful communication. This presupposes that the fundamental categories of behaviour are absolute and our own.

Stage 4: Acceptance

This is when we genuinely acknowledge cultural difference and see that difference within its own cultural context, although we do not necessarily like or agree with it. However, we are curious and question in order to be informed, rather than rely on prejudices.

Stage 5: Adaptation

When individuals change their own attitudes, behaviours and even language to match their surroundings in an attempt to communicate and empathize. This is the ability to act properly outside of our own culture.

Stage 6: Integration

Individuals move freely between cultures; they have a definition of self that is marginal (not central) to any particular culture, allowing the individual to shift smoothly from one cultural world view to another.

Once you have travelled, the voyage never ends, but is played out over and over again in the quietest chambers. The mind can never break off from the journey.

Pat Conroy

---

3 The Diversity Dashboard

... Much more important is to build a matrix in the manager's mind so that he or she sees the world in terms of the tensions, conflicts and trade-offs that are part of operating in today's world.

Christopher A. Bartlett

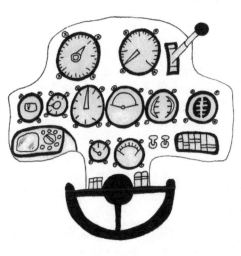

The Diversity Dashboard shows you just how complex the real world of work is and what myriad world views there are. It is the main feature in the cultural cockpit. There are fifteen different instruments that you can use to assess the cultures you are working with. Work with each instrument to understand what aspect of culture in the workplace it is assessing and then calibrate how your way of working misses, mixes or matches that of others.

They have been specially designed to guide you on your journey. They are not prescriptive. They are just tools for you to gauge your assumptions, beliefs and values. They allow you to compare and contrast your methods with others. Determine your own cultural profile, and accept that conflicting viewpoints are inevitable in an international context. The fifteen instruments to assess cross-cultural differences in the work place are:

1. Initiative: individual or group

2. Management: equality or hierarchy

3. Leadership: got or given

4. Communication: direct or indirect

5. Trade: deal or relationship

6. Decisions: head or heart

7. Planning: goal-focused, work–life balance or ad hoc

8. Productivity: effective, efficient or empathetic

9. Rules: rigid or flexible

10. Time: deadline or sometime

11. Style: formal or informal

12. Risk: do or don't

13. Trust: open or closed

14. Gender: inclusive or differentiated

15. Resilience: face or no face

The instruments work on the notion of comparison, whereby the values in one culture or society are compared to those in other cultures or societies. How they measure up on the instruments is relative. Culture only exists by comparison.

It is important to note that the value one society holds as being positive or good in their cultural context can be experienced negatively by someone else because they view things differently. The critical incidents or 'culture crashes' following the description of each instrument demonstrate this.

Note: These instruments are based on the theoretical underpinning of research done by Edward T. Hall, Geert Hofstede, Fons Trompenaars, Charles Hampden-Turner, Richard D. Lewis and others.

Don't lose sight of who you are

One of our interviewees stated, 'Trying to adapt to other cultures and keep my own identity can be confusing.' The challenge is finding what is right for you in the situation you are in – after you have assessed your own assumptions.

Our assumptions derive from the values and beliefs we have about how an organization should work, and our behaviours derive from how we think we can succeed in that workplace – and so we become the manger we are. Recognizing and adapting to cultural diversity should never involve losing contact with your own set of values and behaviours. What we should be aiming for is the ability to live with complexity, to live without being judgemental – not 'this is right and that is wrong' but to hold that all ways are valid even though they are 'not mine'. Eventually we accept the world is full of difference and there are multiple world views.

This is in line with the final 'A' to get your wings: action – the willingness to adapt and be flexible, and the ability to identify and respond creatively to cultural challenges and conflicts in ways that both respect and engage the other person.

...The challenge is to have the willingness to confront our own assumptions, to question them, and to hold on to the essential ones out of a sense of conviction rather than a fear of something different.

Schneider and Barsoux

Confidence booster

Cultural intelligence is clearly more than just learning to tolerate behaviour you feel uncomfortable with. It is about understanding the different value sets of others and the beliefs underlying their behaviour, even though they seem strange to you. Your task is to manage at work with these differences in mind. Our task is to give you the tools and a set of realistic expectations in order for you to manage successfully.

Initiative: individual or group

Misunderstood national culture differences have been cited as the most important factors behind the failure rate of global JVs and alliances.

Piero Morosini

---

individual														**team**
Anglo	Germanic	Nordic		Latin European		Israel		China	Latin America	India	Brazil	Near Eastern	East Africa	West Africa	Far Eastern	Russian	Arab

This instrument compares how people relate to each other. Our research indicates this instrument has the greatest cultural influences on behaviour in the workplace.

In America, the possibility of individual self-realization is the central goal of its civilization. In contrast, the Japanese term for a mature individual translates as a 'person among others'. In China, what we see as taking the initiative can be viewed as immaturity – you have not yet grown up enough to think about the needs of the group.

31

Western theories of motivation have individuals growing ... into an individually resplendent self-actualization at the summit of the hierarchy. Needless to say, this does not achieve resonance the world over, however good a theory it may be for the USA and northwest Europe. The Japanese notion of the highest good is harmonious relationships within and with the patterns of nature; the primary orientation is to other people and to the natural world.

Trompenaars & Hampden-Turner

Culture crash

The conference was looming and yet no marketing had taken place. The board was concerned that the event would make a loss. The new president (British) of this international organization took it upon herself to create a temporary promotional website. She thought this would help to move the project forward as the delay of the official website was becoming an issue.

On Sunday night, as she hit the email send button informing her colleagues they would be able to start marketing from Monday morning; she felt that, as a newbie, she had made a considerable contribution to the organization with her helpful actions. When Monday morning arrived, she was dismayed to find that she had managed to alienate half the board. Her inbox was filled with angry or resentful notes from Bulgaria, Hungary, Spain and Poland asking who had given her the authority to take such a step. The past president (American) sent her a congratulatory note for a job well done.

Culture tip

The British are highly pragmatic. They focus on 'what are we trying to achieve?' In the president's culture, taking the initiative and making things happen are commendable. Being able to side step and get around roadblocks to achieve an outcome is highly valued and not uncommon (Americans are similar). When faced with a problem that she realized she could easily solve, the president went ahead. She never considered that it would be a wrong move. However, rather than being seen as helpful, her actions were seen by the more group-oriented members as unprincipled and maverick. For them, matters need to be decided consensually. The president's actions, at the extreme, were seen as being typical of British imperialism – she was riding roughshod over everyone else, imposing her way and ignoring the feelings of others.

In talking of the Japanese, one manager stated: '…things happen because they have teams; because they have teams that stay together. Longevity of a team is very important to success, and the ability to maintain that bond, that knowledge sharing, through people is extremely important.'

In societies that favour the individual, such as the president's in the story above, people believe they are responsible for their own destinies and actions. Successful people show ambition and initiative. They work hard, take risks and are quick to seize opportunities.

These individualistic cultures place a high regard on a person's ability to think outside the box, and encourage people to have their own opinions and ideas. Individualistic cultures do not want standard knowledge; they want interpreted knowledge, distilled wisdom and fresh insights, all of which are highly individualized. And they want people to take action. Direct feedback, rewards and recognition based on individual performance are all expected.

People emphasize their achievements, positions and personal wealth; this is what gives them their self-esteem. They strive for more and to gain better jobs, always climbing the corporate ladder to success. 'Getting there' is more important than forging good relationships. Status symbols in the form of homes, cars and other forms of conspicuous consumption are accepted. Failure is acceptable, but not passivity. Bankruptcy is a legal process, not a cause for guilt and shame. 'Moonlighting', holding more than one job or having a business on the side of a day job, is common.

'Western corporates often undertake team-building sessions. To them a team is a collection of individuals bought together for a purpose and who need to learn how to work together as a cohesive group.'

Culture crash

A British company was due to draw up a new contract with a German-based company. The night before submission Peter, the manager of the English company, was flying back from the Middle East. His flight was cancelled. Unfortunately his phone battery died, causing problems for his team back in the manufacturing plant in Costa Rica.

Without any communication from Peter in twenty-four hours, one member of his team, an American lady, Jane, took it upon herself to make sure that the contract was delivered. Her colleagues, two Costa Rican men who were new to the company, were not so sure about this proactive stance. They made it clear that the contract should be finalized only when Peter was there to review it. Jane thought differently. She felt it was her responsibility to make sure the contract was delivered by that afternoon, which it was. She knew the Germans would see their failure to deliver as being unreliable.

Late that evening, Peter arrived back. He checked his emails, which contained a copy of the contract that had been sent. His relief on seeing that the contract had been sent out in time changed to dismay when he viewed some of the details. Although he was aggrieved that the margins were not as good as they could have been, he had to acknowledge that the company operated a 'no blame' culture and that the priority had been to submit the contract on time. Peter called a meeting early the next morning. He quickly realized that the Costa Ricans were thinking that 'Americans aren't team players; they do things for personal glory'.

Culture tip

Costa Ricans have a low score for individuality; they are more concerned about the team as a whole. The element of loyalty to the group is paramount and Jane's actions were definitely not team-oriented – in their view. She used her initiative and took the situation into her own hands because she understood the importance of first impressions with the German company, and that on-time delivery was important to them. Members of highly individualistic cultures are very self-reliant and action-oriented. Achievement and outcome are their main focus. When it comes to the concept of individual versus group, it really boils down to the difference between 'I' and 'we'.

People from many cultures, including the Costa Ricans, need to work collectively as a group with a focus on maintaining face. Seizing the initiative is frowned upon. Group orientation means members within that society, from birth onwards, are integrated into cohesive communities which, throughout a member's lifetime, continue to protect them in exchange for unflinching loyalty.

Guatemala and Egypt are amongst the most group-oriented cultures. Asian cultures, such as China, view other countries with less of a group philosophy as cold and non-supportive. These cultures emphasize the community and think more in terms of 'we' and 'us'. Questioning and challenging an authority figure or established wisdom is seen to be disrespectful. Knowledge is being an understander of the people around you, not of things. Group learning and knowledge sharing are important. Standing out in the crowd as a prominent individual is culturally unacceptable. At work, employees value common interests, conformity, cooperation and interdependence – they don't have to practice team-building; they live and breathe it.

The Japanese turns to his boss and says, 'That was absolutely brilliant. When I get home I am going to take that idea and improve it.' The American turns to his boss and says, 'That was pretty good, but I have a much better idea I am going to try when I get home.'

Dr. Peter Cochrane, formerly head of BT's Innovation Centre

Culture crash

In the global downturn, with sales sluggish, the US parent company of a Swedish operations division announced a twelve per cent budget cut on expenses. Lars, the Swedish director from manufacturing, Antonio, the Italian director from marketing and a third from sales, an America called Chris, were tasked with recommending where to make the cuts.

The three directors met; they grumbled and pointed out all the difficulties. The discussion began to get fraught as each director took a very different stance. As a way forward, Lars suggested the reduction be split evenly across the three divisions: that was only fair. Antonio passionately pitched for no reduction whatsoever: it would bring too much hardship. Chris argued that it was only through increased sales revenue that the problem would be solved and suggested the other two divisions absorb the cut. He further proposed that the other two departments take a greater cut and those savings be passed on to the sales division. The result: impasse.

Culture tip

Americans, favouring action and achievement, believe initiative should be rewarded. High salaries/bonuses for salespeople are part of this go-getting culture. Swedes are more moderate and realize that nobody can do a job without the support of others, and in this respect believe in fare shares. The Italians are group-oriented and more emotional, and so relate to matters like these with their feelings.

Cultural insight

A business graduate we know was on the lookout for a new job. He is ambitious and wanted to start his career on the right foot. He'd searched relentlessly on the internet for positions in HR and whittled down the list to two companies and locations. Catching his eye were Germany and Indonesia, and the companies sent through job specifications for him.

For the position in Germany, he had been given a fully detailed job description, including job title, background on the company, what the person would be expected to do, responsibilities and reporting, experience required, qualifications and skills required, personal attributes that would fit the profile. For the Indonesian position, the outline he received was quite vague – a job title and overview of the position and duties. He believes that the networking possibilities and the very different cultural experience of Indonesia would benefit him in the long run. He feels that the position is for him; however, he does not know exactly what is required from him. So how can he choose between the two jobs?

Organizations in individualistic societies give very precise job descriptions so that those applying understand exactly what they are supposed to achieve in the role. HR's function is to do a detailed breakdown of the job and determine ways to monitor and measure performance against those criteria. In group-oriented societies, job descriptions are deliberately left vague; there is no point in being prescriptive as the reality of the role is about bending and flexing with those around you.

Story

One of our contributors to this book, a diplomat from the Middle East, commented 'Debby, the thing you don't really understand about us is how lonely it is to live in UK. Where I come from, all week we are planning what to do on Fridays, at the weekends, with our families. And, by that, we don't mean just our wives and children. We involve our whole family – brothers, cousins, parents, sisters. We are a community. We are always socializing with each other. And then I came here… Yes, I have friends in the diplomatic mission and we socialize with work. But, I feel empty inside. It is as though I've been tossed into a vast ocean without a life raft…' This must feel dreadful and will surely affect productivity, so when working across cultures do be sensitive to colleagues from those different cultures.

Confidence booster

When you work with other cultures words like' table' or 'chair' are easily understood. Much more difficult are concepts such as 'initiative', 'late' or 'as soon as possible'. Be sure you check your understanding with other people's.

Creating cultural confidence

Whilst reading this book why not capture your insights and possible action steps as they occur to you? Use the spaces below to record your ideas regarding your relationships with yourself, your team, your clients and your organization.

Your relationship with yourself

Insights   Actions

_____   _____
_____   _____
_____   _____
_____   _____

Your relationship with the team

Insights   Actions

_____   _____
_____   _____
_____   _____
_____   _____

Your relationship with clients

Insights   Actions

_____   _____
_____   _____
_____   _____
_____   _____

Your relationship with the organization

Insights   Actions

_____   _____
_____   _____
_____   _____
_____   _____

5 Management: equality or hierarchy

The hierarchical nature of Indian society demands that there is a boss and that the boss should be seen to be the boss. Everyone else just does as they are told, and even if they know the boss is 100% wrong, no one will argue.

Gitanjali Kolanad

equality   hierarchy

Nordic Germanic	Anglo	Israel	Latin European	Japan	East Africa	India	Brazil	West Africa	Latin America	Near Eastern	Far Eastern	Arab	Russian

Within almost every organization there is a hierarchy among the employees based on position, title, role, and function. In some sense, hierarchical distinctions create a class system in the workplace. Depending on your attitude to egalitarianism this may cause some employees to feel like 'somebodies' and others to feel like 'nobodies'. This instrument compares the degree of acceptance of unequal power distribution – or the power distance (small or large) between those in charge and their less powerful employees.

Rank is an important and necessary tool in the management of organizations. In societies that are more egalitarian, within the area where it has been earned, rank deserves and commands respect. However, in these societies people like and need to be treated as equals to perform well. Western management practice has to find ways for participation: recognizing the work that each employee contributes, including lower-level employees in major organizational social events, avoiding unnecessary distinctions that may make certain groups feel like second-class citizens, providing opportunities for employees at lower ranks to offer suggestions about how to do their work better, and including employees of differing ranks on committees and task forces, where appropriate.

One international manager we interviewed remarked: 'People in the Far East are brought up to fear making a mistake, as this would bring a reprimand from a superior in the hierarchy. So, they've grown up to be both fearful and respectful of their superiors.'

Culture crash

A pharmaceutical firm in Sweden decided to undergo a joint venture in the Middle East. A Saudi Arabian was appointed as divisional director with a German expat as his number two. A recent trip to Saudi Arabia by the Swedish CEO did not go well when he witnessed every decision that needed to be made being passed up the chain of command and, worse still, there were times when people waited to be told what to do. He considered the ease and flow of information being passed between the various departments in Sweden, and how each department was allowed to make decisions based on what they knew best. 'Why is this not happening over here?' he demanded.

Culture tip

In many hierarchical countries, including Saudi Arabia, the boss is the boss. Employees expect authority figures to manage and supervise them, and instruct them about what to do. In Sweden, the workers in a company are able to approach their managers. In fact the term 'manager' is hardly used, as they view their managers more as coaches and mentors; for them, organizations consist of a gathering of equals. For Swedes, being instructed in how to do something can cause embarrassment, and being micro-managed will more than likely cause a lack of motivation for the job. German expatriates, used to German organizational hierarchy, are comfortable with titles and structure; however, like the Swedes, they hate to be micro-managed. Tell them the goal to be achieved and leave them alone to work on it.

In egalitarian cultures, people are trained to be competent in their role and delegation of responsibility can therefore be passed down the ranks. The Finns, Norwegians, Swedes and Dutch are amongst the most egalitarian cultures with extremely flat management structures. The boss is regarded as an equal, participation is expected, opinions can be expressed openly, you can tell a boss that they are misguided or even wrong. Employees expect a consultative approach to decision making. Employee initiative is valued and expected. Generally it is more important to get the work done than to go through the right channels.

In hierarchical countries, such as China, people expect the use and application of management authority and decisiveness. Seniors are expected to tell juniors what to do. For these cultures, knowledge is seen as being the manifestation of the status of a person – it's not what you know but who you know. Employees do not contradict or challenge their superiors in the hierarchy as a superior is viewed as a teacher or dispenser of wisdom and given much respect. With officialdom, bureaucrats are always right regardless of what they say. In practice this means employees do not try to get above themselves and when something goes wrong the responsibility claims people higher up the ladder. The president or even the whole board might resign. Responsibility comes with the status of being the boss and not with the (in)competent person, as in more egalitarian organizations.

Culture crash

David, a British banking manager, was supervising an Indian trainee, Rakesh. Rakesh was delighted to be in London to collaborate on projects. David was pleased to be able to push work to Rakesh who worked diligently, but he still seemed to crave guidance. After two months, believing that Rakesh could now stand on his own two feet, David gave him a couple of projects with tight deadlines to complete on his own.

'Let me know if you run into any problems,' David said as he retreated into his office. Several days went past and Rakesh made little progress and seemed somewhat unhappy. He confided in a friend that he thought he must have offended his boss. 'I will have to work twice as hard on my next project,' he admitted.

Culture tip

Rakesh expects his boss to stay close and guide him – like a father figure. Checking in with David ensures proper process and shares the responsibility in case something goes wrong. When David distances himself, Rakesh thinks it is because he has somehow disappointed or offended him; what other reason could there be?

Culture crash

Shirley, a British HR manager, has just transferred to Singapore. She has a warm and friendly personality and soon establishes rapport with the workforce. As time goes by she hears the staff making complaints about some of the work practices and so arranges a formal meeting with the boss so they can air their grievances. To her surprise and embarrassment, when given the opportunity, none of the staff speak up, some even saying, 'There's nothing to complain about'.

Culture tip

As a Brit, Shirley expects to share her concerns with her boss if things are not going as well as they could. She would even expect to enter into a discussion about improvements or even to challenge her boss's decision if she felt the need. Dissension and disagreement are allowed and expected. In Singapore, employees are more rule-abiding and will maintain a harmonious environment despite work disagreements. Authority knows best. Employees operate on a principle of unquestioning adherence to dictates by senior management.

Culture crash

The American division of a Japanese electronics company receives its new Japanese vice president of sales. As part of his new regime, the VP states that every morning the sales team will start the day with a team conference call about the prospecting opportunities for the coming couple of days. He says he also requires more detailed and more frequent reports concerning how sales leads are progressing. The 'salesman of the month' bonus scheme is to be ended and the money will be distributed to reflect a more team approach. Dan Bradshaw, one of the company's leading sales executives, decides to look for another job: 'What, doesn't he trust me or something? I'm not going to be micro-managed like that!'

One interviewee remarked: 'In many Asian countries, you have to micro-manage to a degree that you would never have imagined possible back in the UK.'

Culture tip

In a hierarchical culture, an egalitarian and participative preference can be interpreted by staff as a lack of competence and confidence in your own decisions. Equally, an egalitarian-oriented person may feel that their subordinates in a hierarchical organization lack initiative. If you are supervising someone whose preference for power distance is higher than yours, you will need to provide him or her with much more direction and oversight than you would like from your own supervisor. In dealing with seniors, you will need to take steps to adjust your style to cultures where inequalities among people are both expected and desired. Asian companies tend to be led by strong authoritarian figures who take a very active role in daily operations.

Cultural insight

The Japanese do not consider private offices appropriate: only the highest ranking officers have private offices, and may have desks in large work areas as well.

Cultural insight

Western workers may well state a preference for egalitarian social structures but there remains an enduring preference for hierarchy. People like structure and they like to know how they fit within the organization chart or chain of command. However, it has to be hierarchy 'the right way'. Employees perceive a lack of fairness as mistreatment, which results in lower levels of job satisfaction and performance, and lower levels of loyalty and commitment to the organization. Resentment builds as they feel that they are not being given dignity and respect.

Confidence booster

Always establish the facts before making an assessment, jumping to conclusions or making assumptions based on your personal position on the Diversity Dashboard. Over-confidence can get you into awkward situations.

Cultural competence check

When a cultural conflict occurs, the best way to resolve it is to insist on maintaining one's own values and arguing for their logical validity, while letting the other party do the same. Rational persuasion is the best way to resolve the conflict. True or False?

Answer

False. While a clear statement of values may be a starting point for a discussion, it is often necessary to understand the history, geography and economics that lie behind them. Each culture has a story that can remain hidden if the only dialogue is rational persuasion.

Creating cultural confidence

Whilst reading this book why not capture your insights and possible action steps as they occur to you? Use the spaces below to record your ideas regarding your relationships with yourself, your team, your clients and your organization.

Your relationship with yourself

Insights   Actions

_____   _____
_____   _____
_____   _____
_____   _____

Your relationship with the team

Insights   Actions

_____   _____
_____   _____
_____   _____
_____   _____

Your relationship with clients

Insights   Actions

_____   _____
_____   _____
_____   _____
_____   _____

Your relationship with the organization

Insights   Actions

_____   _____
_____   _____
_____   _____
_____   _____

6 Leadership: got or given

> For a Spaniard, success lies in the titles as much as in the salary, and much more than in the work.
>
> **Helen Wattley Ames**

got   given

| Anglos | Nordics | Nigeria | Germanics | Latin Europe | West Africa | Far East | India | Russia | Brazil | Latin America | East Africa | Arab |

Leadership is a process by which a person influences others to accomplish an objective and directs the organization in a way that makes it more cohesive and coherent. But who do you allow to influence you? Who do you look up to? Who do you esteem? Who is an authority figure in your eyes? In the workplace, who is the boss and how did they become the boss? And to what extent is your boss superior to you? Different cultures confer status on individuals in different ways and this instrument compares the way in which a society gives certain members higher status than others.

Americans want so much to get to the top or make a corporate name for themselves that they scarcely take time out for their families, for recreation or for pleasure.

The view of a Mexican manager

Culture crash

In a former job as a high-flying banker, Derek Arden, past president of the Professional Speaking Association (PSA) and one of our professional-speaking friends, was sent to Korea as a troubleshooter to rescue negotiations. Previously two of his colleagues had seen the deal deteriorate and returned empty-handed to the UK. As soon as Derek entered the meeting he knew why. Before him sat a group of eight mature Korean gentlemen. He was the lone representative from England. 'It was enough to make anyone quake in their shoes,' he explained. 'No wonder my colleagues felt overwhelmed.'

Culture tip

Some societies accord leadership to people on the basis of their achievements and their track record – i.e. what they have done. In other words, they've achieved it through their own efforts and 'got' it. Anglo-Saxon, North American and north-western European cultures believe that assigning status for reasons other than achievement is archaic and inappropriate to business. These societies are meritorious and people are promoted for competence. In the story above, the lone Englishman was given the authority to negotiate on behalf of his bank as a competent individual. Unfortunately, the Koreans interpreted this as a slight: if a well-respected large British bank were really interested in doing business with them, then surely they would have sent many senior people and not simply one solitary manager?

Culture crash

After eight years away at a US business school and then working for a global microprocessor manufacturer, Hong Yen returns to take up a position as an expat manager in China. At 35, he is significantly younger than other senior international managers. In addition, few Chinese nationals hold such powerful positions in multinational companies in China.

When meeting with officials, especially from local government, Hong Yen had difficulty persuading them that he was directly authorized to make decisions. He found his opinions and suggestions were not taken seriously and that the officials had little confidence in him. As a ploy, he invented a boss and would tell the officials 'I should speak with my boss' whilst also giving his own opinion. Over time, the officials noticed that Hong Yen's opinions matched those of his boss and he was able to establish trust and credibility.

Culture tip

Some societies assign status to people by virtue of who they are based on age, class, gender, education, profession, social connections and family (i.e. who they are is important). Their status relies on the connections they have and the network of knowledge they can tap into. The older they are, the more grey hairs they have (and often whether they are male), the more they are esteemed. Leadership has been bestowed or 'given' to them. So much deference can be paid to these persons of importance that, even outside of the working environment, they have sway, influence and superiority. They are authority figures who are not to be questioned and carry full responsibility for the actions of their subordinates. In the case above, Hong Yen was given the job because he was competent in the eyes of his US multinational, but for his peers in Beijing he was too young to be of consequence.

At work, in achievement-oriented, leadership-got cultures, knowledge and competence go together. Therefore authority can be delegated to any competent person – 'whomever of a lower rank'. Situational leadership is a reflection of this culture: a leader may pass total control and authority of a project to someone because they are better qualified/ more competent / have the knowledge for the task, and then assume leadership again once the task has been completed. However, this contrasts starkly with leadership-given societies.

Culture crash

The Indian engineer had been chosen to accompany the visiting Finnish electronics engineer as he travelled around the company's plants in India demonstrating how to assemble their latest mobile phones. He was to learn the job and take on the role of senior supervisor in Delhi. At each stage of the process, the Finnish engineer would enquire whether his Indian colleague had followed the instruction and understood what to do. In reply, the Indian would nod enthusiastically and say, 'Oh yes, Sir.' On the very last visit, the Finn turned to the Indian and said, 'Now it's your turn. You demonstrate how to do it too.' Unfortunately, the Indian remained silent and averted his eyes; he was unable to do the task.

Culture tip

In egalitarian, leadership-got societies, competence comes from questioning, action learning and asking outright when you do not understand. The Finn expected his Indian counterpart to speak up if he didn't understand something. As someone who comes from a hierarchical culture where leadership is given, the Indian engineer would find it difficult to question his teacher on three counts: first, the teacher is a god-like figure and questioning a teacher challenges existing wisdom; secondly, he didn't want to lose face and admit he didn't understand; thirdly, he could not ask questions because that would mean he had not understood what was said, and that would mean his teacher would lose face – i.e. what the teacher had said had not been clear enough. But the teacher is always right. A better way for the Indian to learn would have been for the Finn to give him the opportunity to discuss and learn within his peer group.

Culture challenge: Who would you choose?

Job description: *Director of marketing, largest fishing corporation based in St Louis in Senegal.*

Key role: *To create a plan for new international markets.*

Important factor: *Successful applicant will be required to recruit staff and spend three months training in Boston, US.*

Short-listed candidates:

- Applicant A: a married lady in her mid-forties with four children. She comes from a polygamist family. Her half-brother is the current chief of their village. She studied in France a number of years ago. She does not speak English. She recently went on pilgrimage to Mecca where she earned the title of Al Hadja. Her husband is the judge of the Appeals Court in St Louis.

- Applicant B: a single lady with no children. Her father is the powerful mayor of St Louis. She speaks fluent English and French and is computer literate. She studied business at a major US college. Being fluent in English, she will benefit more from the training in Boston and her language skills will be a great advantage for translating documents and when dealing with new international clients.

The executive team cannot decide on which applicant to choose. The position remains open after four months. Who would you select and why?

Cultural insight

You could support the youthful and dynamic Applicant B. She should be open to new ideas and her language skills, experience of studying in America plus her IT skills are a great asset to any international company. On the face of it, she is the more competent candidate. But is she too young? Candidate A, on the other hand, is more mature with the responsibility of caring for family and community – very important in Senegalese culture. She brings the advantage of a professional husband who may be able to assist the company with legal matters. She is well connected and her pilgrimage to Mecca ensures that she is well respected. In this culture, her age, status as a married woman with lots of children and her religious devotion will engender unquestioning obedience from her subordinates. But how will she manage being in Boston for three months?

Confidence booster

Few people take offence when genuine mistakes are made. However, when things get tough or continually go wrong you tend to revert to your own worst stereotypes. Don't take things personally; reach out and put yourself in the other's shoes. Get a different perspective. See a diverse world full of interesting opportunities.

Creating cultural confidence

Whilst reading this book why not capture your insights and possible action steps as they occur to you? Use the spaces below to record your ideas regarding your relationships with yourself, your team, your clients and your organization.

Your relationship with yourself

Insights   Actions

_____   _____
_____   _____
_____   _____
_____   _____

Your relationship with the team

Insights   Actions

_____   _____
_____   _____
_____   _____
_____   _____

Your relationship with clients

Insights   Actions

_____   _____
_____   _____
_____   _____
_____   _____

Your relationship with the organization

Insights   Actions

_____   _____
_____   _____
_____   _____
_____   _____

7 Communication: direct or indirect

If any man were to ask me what would I suppose to be the perfect style of language, I would answer, that in which a man speaking to five hundred people, of all common and various capacities, idiots and lunatics excepted, should be understood by them all, and in the same sense which the speaker intended to be understood.

Daniel Defoe

direct												indirect
Finns	Nordics	Dutch	Germanic	Anglos	British	French	Russian	Latin European	Latin American	Indian	Arab	Far Eastern

COMMUNICATION
DIRECT — INDIRECT

Communication is how you do and say things – and why, when other people do and say things differently, you notice. Sometimes you mind, and sometimes you don't. It takes a combination of good self-awareness, cross-cultural knowledge and sensitivity to be effective across cultures. If you want to get on in business across the globe, ensure you research and study the countries you will be speaking with. Understand the values of the country, what makes them tick and, above all, how they communicate. Do they speak frankly (direct) or do they hint (indirect) at what they mean?

Culture crash

One of our speaking colleagues who frequently travels on business often uses a translator for his speeches. After one such presentation, he learned that the Chinese interpreter's version of his opening remarks went like this: 'The highly respected media expert is beginning his speech with a thing called a joke. I am not sure why, but many Australians believe it necessary to start a speech with a joke. [Pause] He is telling a joke now, but frankly you would not understand this joke, so I will not translate it. He thinks I am telling you the joke now. The polite thing to do when he finishes is to laugh. [Pause] He is getting close. [Pause] Esteemed speaker has just told the joke. Laugh – now!'

The audience not only laughed appreciatively but stood and applauded as well. Our colleague later commented to the translator, 'I've been giving speeches for years and you are the first translator who knows how to tell a good joke.' The translator answered, 'Your joke was rather rude plus I do not think the students would have understood it, so I just told them to laugh at the appropriate point!'

Culture tip

Humour does not translate well between cultures, especially between indirect and direct cultures. Some nations, like the northern Europeans and the Japanese, like facts and figures while others, such as the Americans, like lots of emotional appeal and often open their presentations with a joke. It would be a mistake to use the American style and approach in northern Europe, and vice versa. Always stay in safe and familiar territory, as many a deal and relationship has been spoiled due to lack of understanding and poor judgement. Your objective is always to be clearly understood in the way you intended.

When it comes to language, native English speakers use a lot of colloquial expressions that are meaningless to other nations. For example, a colleague went to Russia and used the expression, 'out of sight, out of mind'; the Russians translated it as 'blind idiot'. So it makes sense to avoid such expressions. 'Knocked for six', 'a level playing field' or 'a ball-park figure' do not translate well. Not everyone knows baseball or cricket and colloquialisms get in the way of clear communication. Keep it straightforward and simple. Do not assume that popular mnemonic such as KISS (for keep it short and sweet) will work either. In fact, do not assume anything!

Communication in Arab culture is subtle, indirect and non-verbal. Indeed, it is customary for Arabs to use terms and phrases that have double meanings, descend from the very general to the specific, start a conversation with small talk, go around and about an issue, call upon proverbs and poetic expressions and speak with their face, eyes and hands.

Jamil Hammoud

Even when you aim to get it right, you can get aspects wrong. You must look at the fundamental values of each culture and tailor what you want to say to match it. People from egalitarian 'I' and 'me' cultures prefer clarity in their conversations in order to communicate more effectively and directly. Directness is seen as honest and showing respect by treating others as equals. It is expected that this directness will be reciprocated. Conflict is seen as opportunity as long as it is dealt with openly and rationally. In business and work situations, hesitancy may be interpreted as hiding something or as insincerity.

Cultural insight

Visitors to the United States may be surprised to find that arguments seem focused on winning, with little or no effort toward maintaining harmony or recognizing or deferring to the status or sensibilities of the others involved. US Americans may appear to use phony smiles and be too animated, and the need to always express things in positive terms may be interpreted as naiveté. They also tend to speak loudly to show enthusiasm, and feel being positive and optimistic avoids needless confrontation and gets the best results in both work and life. They tend to be animated, outgoing, use facial expressions and considerable eye contact. They are uncomfortable with silences. An overriding value is to speak up and voice opinions.

Culture crash

John, an American, was on a conference call to Prakesh in India. He said, 'This proposal is poorly prepared. Have it re-done by 15.00 hours tomorrow, Saturday.' Prakesh was upset and complained about John's rudeness to his team leader, and asked for a transfer to a department where he would report to a native Indian.

Culture tip

We were called into support with cultural training. We explained the difference between straight talking and indirect communication. The latter allows the possibility for saving face, shame or embarrassment for both sides. 'Looks like this piece of work will need to be finished during the weekend,' is a more indirect way of saying, 'You need to work on Saturday!' or 'Can you work on Saturday?' The challenge is the mismatch of words and expectations. When a direct manager listens to an indirect employee he may think the person is taking a long time to get to the point or even being deliberately awkward and obscure. The opposite is true for indirect communicators, who see straight talking as rude and aggressive.

You see, direct communicators sound authoritarian and are often perceived as insensitive. If you work for them, they do not hesitate to tell you what to do and when to do it. Meanings are explicit and on the surface. They are driven by a strong sense of 'now'. They are often in a hurry to get the job done. They get to the bottom line quickly and don't have much patience with those who, in their opinion, beat around the bush. They are frequently brutally honest in their interactions. They are comfortable expressing their emotions outwardly, and do so routinely. They look people in the eye and, if this is not returned, they are suspicious, lacking trust. In western cultures communication is explicit, direct and unambiguous.

Culture crash

Margot Kind was visiting Singapore to do business with a Chinese Malay garment factory. At the negotiation stage her counterparts fell silent. Margot explained, 'The Chinese representatives just went very quiet. It was unnerving. Even with my cultural training I found it very hard to relax and be still as they completed their quiet deliberations. It seemed to take forever.'

Culture tip

Many people fail to appreciate the meaning of silence. In intercultural communication it is an important part of proceedings; silences are not necessarily an absence of communication and are often a part of it. Asians wait longer before they speak, especially to someone in authority. Indirect communicators from Asian cultures believe that it is better to talk too little than too much. Their use of silence is a good indication of their power or position. The bold response in the indirect world is a rude response. In Malaysia (and Asia), silences can be a sign of respect; in Japan, negotiators use it as a way to control the negotiation process; in Finland, it is a way of encouraging a speaker to continue.

It is virtually impossible for a direct communicator to fully understand the complexities of indirectness until they have been immersed in it. There are a lot of non-verbal messages that get missed entirely. If you are a direct communicator, you need to slow down, learn how to listen empathetically and to discover the power of storytelling to convey meaning. Direct communicators believe they are responsible for reshaping and repeating what they say until it is understood in the way they intended. Indirect communicators use parables, storytelling and little sayings to convey meaning rather than give an outright message; it's down to the listener to interpret what is meant. It's almost as though you have to listen for what is not being said.

Indirect communicators are really very interesting if you take time to study them. Communication is about sensitivity to another person's feelings and as these people value courtesy highly they will always seek out the polite response and be hesitant to give bad news. They will find a way to avoid directly answering a question by changing the subject to indicate disagreement, saying 'it will be difficult'. They will leave sentences unfinished and not admit a lack of understanding. They will frequently tell a story and allow listeners to come to their own conclusions. Meanings are implicit and embedded. They conceal their emotions and avoid a direct gaze, as they feel it is aggressive and disrespectful to make eye contact.

Cultural insight

For Americans, Brits and north-western Europeans there is the concept of truth being an absolute – black and white – but not so in the rest of the world! They have no difficulty in saying 'yes' or 'no', words which are meant to be taken at face value. They do not make false but friendly promises in order to get along with someone; if they promise, they deliver. Their trading partners, such as Mexicans, Indians and people from the Middle East and Asia, need to understand the significance of the commitments they make from the direct communicators' standpoint. Indirect communicators say 'yes' very quickly – and this 'yes' is believed to mean 'yes'. For indirect cultures, a well-intentioned word is an acceptable substitute for action. They sometimes lack a strong commitment for what they say they are going to do. They do not feel disgraced if problems cause delay or prevent the agreed outcome.

Americans, especially, make notes on conversations, keep files, record minutes of meetings. Contracts or agreements must be written before business is taken seriously. However, in indirect cultures 'getting it in writing' is considered rude.

Cultural compass

In indirect cultures there are many alternatives designed to deflect awkwardness or embarrassment. If you hear any of the following, the person is probably trying to say 'no':

1. Your question is very difficult to answer…
2. If everything goes as planned, the proposal will be approved…
3. Have you submitted a copy of your proposal to…?
4. It is difficult to answer this question at this time…
5. Will you be staying longer than you planned?
6. Yes, approval looks likely, but…
7. You should know shortly…

Cultural compass

Ten strategies for clear cross-cultural communication:

1. Speak slowly and clearly.
2. Ask for clarification or summarize your understanding of what has been said.
3. Frequently check for others' understanding.
4. Avoid idioms, metaphors and other colloquialisms.
5. Cut out jargon.
6. Clearly define your business concepts – e.g. what does 'as soon as possible' mean?
7. Be specific.
8. Choose your medium of communication effectively.
9. Provide information via multiple channels.
10. Be patient.

Cultural competence check

True or false?

Using humorous anecdotes is a way of breaking the ice and establishing a relaxed atmosphere prior to getting down to business in international meetings.

True or false?

During management training with a session full of different nationalities, Scandinavian delegates are more than willing to join in with the role-play part.

Confidence booster

Confusion occurs when you lack awareness of your own communication style and project it on others. In the absence of better knowledge, you tend to assume. Instead, find out what an action means – for example, a straight look into the other person's face, as in the UK, is regarded as disrespectful in Japan.

Humour doesn't travel well. Japanese, Chinese, Germans, Finns all find jokes out of place in business settings. Asian humour finds little merit in jokes about sex, religion or minorities. Many cultures take what is said quite literally and do not understand expressions such as 'You can say that again!'

Answer: False.

Generally speaking Scandinavians do not like to take part in role play; it goes against the grain. They like to be upfront and honest, and role-playing means pretending to be someone that they are not. Respect links to truth and honesty, which then ties in with communication; the Scandinavians are the most direct communicators.

Answer: False

Creating cultural confidence

Whilst reading this book why not capture your insights and possible action steps as they occur to you? Use the spaces below to record your ideas regarding your relationships with yourself, your team, your clients and your organization.

Your relationship with yourself

Insights   Actions

_____   _____
_____   _____
_____   _____
_____   _____

Your relationship with the team

Insights   Actions

_____   _____
_____   _____
_____   _____
_____   _____

Your relationship with clients

Insights   Actions

_____   _____
_____   _____
_____   _____
_____   _____

Your relationship with the organization

Insights   Actions

_____   _____
_____   _____
_____   _____
_____   _____

Trade: deal or relationship

You don't go to a Turk, ask for the price and say 'OK'. You go to a Turk, ask for the price, and then you say, 'But why?'

Uğur Salman

---

deal   relationship

Germanics	Nordics	Anglos	European	Latin America	India	Brazil	Russia	Near Eastern	Arab	East Africa	West Africa	Far Eastern

This instrument compares the degree to which we interact with others in just a commercial or business-only fashion, or to build a relationship. In our interviews with international managers, 85 per cent of the comments were in the context of 'willingness to engage with others'. As Trompenaars and Hampden-Turner (1997) suggest: 'This is not a "waste of time" because such preferences reveal character and form friendships…' which is what is most important in relationship-oriented societies.

Culture crash

One manager talking about his time in the Middle East explained, 'Abdullah said to me, "Brian, I can make this happen for you. I have connections; I can pull strings and know who to ask..."'

Culture tip

As a functional Brit, Brian immediately thought, 'I don't like this. It is underhand, nepotism. I feel uncomfortable.' However, he was to learn that it is the life-blood of business in the Middle East, where relationships matter above everything else.

Doing business with a culture more relationship-oriented than our own can feel time consuming. In such cultures, everything is connected to everything. Your prospective business partner may want to know about your family, your connections, the kinds of food you enjoy and even what you read. Business is done socially and at a much slower pace. People prefer plenty of time to build trust before getting down to business.

Obligations of mutual debt are very strong in such societies and are necessary to make things happen. Such obligations have no boundaries. The English phrase 'you scratch my back and I'll scratch yours' describes this exactly. Mutual-debt societies exist in different forms all over the world. The Japanese *nemawashi* system and the Chinese *guanxi* relationships are forms of the mutual-debt society. However, in the Philippines, the debt or obligation is never absolved; it lasts a lifetime. Their term *utang na loob* means 'sense of being indebted'.

Culture crash

Towards the end of a very pleasant lunch in Paris, Jean Gautier draws his British colleague, Peter Smith, aside and mentions that his teenage son is about to attend a summer school in Surrey in a few months' time. Peter asks a few polite questions and leaves it at that. Two months later, Jean telephones to say his son is on his way and that he would appreciate it if Peter would see that his son is settling in.

Peter is annoyed, thinking 'What's this got to do with me?' However, one Saturday afternoon he takes his own teenage son to visit the young French lad. The boys find they have a passion for rugby in common and agree to keep in touch through Facebook.

Months later, Peter finds that his new reward and recognition initiative for Europe has been completely snubbed by the French. Françoise, the head of HR, has become implacable and won't even return Peter's calls. One day, to his utter amazement, he receives a call from Françoise asking if they could discuss his plans to see how they could adjust them to suit French working practices. When he remarks to a colleague how astounded he was that Françoise had eventually 'seen sense', he learns that Jean Gautier had had 'a quiet word with her'. The time spent with the two teenagers had paid off.

Culture tip

Some societies, like the French, assume there are no boundaries in the business context. That 'little request' may well be for a personal or social favour to a business colleague, thus making business and social spheres overlap or mingle. France is a unique culture where people will only share things with you if you are part of the group. In France there is a network system; they call it *les réseaux* – *réseaux* meaning networks.

Culture crash

Mark, working in China said, 'Asking for something is very problematic – even if it is "objective" knowledge – when you don't understand something and ask. The facts are that you don't know the person, you don't have a relationship with him, you don't have a relationship with the person you're asking. This is seen as an invasion. You need to understand if you have to ask for something.'

Culture tip

Mark explained, 'You don't get what you want in those kinds of cultures until you've done something to justify it happening – even if you are just asking the time!'

In deal-oriented cultures, emotions and relationships are suspect. It is often better *not* to do business with family or friends, if you are in a position of power, in case you are thought to be abusing your position to favour your relatives. 'Favours' and that 'little request' which spill over into the business context are seen as totally inappropriate in the work environment.

Cultural insight

The down-to-business pragmatism of US managers who tend to focus on the bottom line and rely heavily on facts for their business decisions can be misinterpreted by their Mexican counterparts as coldness. 'Mexicans are more informal, less inclined to work with statistics, are more relaxed and "ingenious"', according to Maria Lopez-Bravo. They prefer to know the roots and history of the person they are talking to, and only when a sense of trust develops can the Mexican feel comfortable and ready to do business. Americans view people at work as just colleagues, not as friends. And organizations do not encourage social chat at work. That is not the way a Mexican likes to work.

'The Arab process of building relationships prior to transacting business is very time consuming. However, once a relationship has been established, verbal contracts are absolute and an individual's word is his or her bond and failure to meet verbally agreed obligations will certainly lead to a termination of a business relationship.'

Culture crash

It was Lilja Lappalainen's first visit to South Korea. She was to recruit agents for one of Europe's largest telecom companies and was looking forward to returning to Finland, having recruited a handful of influential people who would make their products fly off the shelves in the Far East. Instead of falling at her feet and rushing to be associated with such a well-known brand, the Koreans seemed to turn every business conversation round to her and pry into her personal life. Back in Helsinki Lilja was dismayed to find that the company had received complaints about her behaviour. She had recruited no agents.

Culture tip

The Finns, like many deal-oriented people, believe that a sound commercial approach to business – one that includes facts, evidence and logic – would be sufficient to persuade any potential Korean candidate to sign up to be an agent. After all, to do business with this prestigious Finnish brand was surely a wise decision. Finnish people are also very private; they are not used to divulging their private lives and would view being questioned about them as a great invasion of privacy.

Contrastingly, the prospective agents needed to expand the business 'life space' of the Finn and wanted to learn about the person with whom they would be dealing – about her background and character. It's all well and good being associated with a famous firm, but in real life it's the relationship with the individual that makes or breaks a deal. The Koreans felt that there was no serious intention of doing business with them as there wasn't any real commitment to getting to know each other and building a relationship.

Both sides had misunderstood the intentions and motives of the other. It was only through our training and intervention that a chasm of misunderstanding was prevented. The deal did not fall through.

Culture crash

Japanese representatives arrived and were shown into the board room of a British-based utilities provider. The CEO, the director for global sales and Darryl, the sales director for Asia-Pac, greeted them warmly. The Brits had prepared well, produced a good-looking brochure on the company, a fact-filled report about how their products and services would fit in the Japanese market and gave a professional PowerPoint presentation. The Japanese, on the other hand, seemed spectacularly unprepared and had to be interrogated to release information about their company.

On being invited to go to Japan to meet with the President of the Japanese business, the CEO replied: 'I'll send my Asia-Pac director, Darryl. Make sure you set up a meeting the next time you are over in the Far East.' 'My president was looking forward to meeting you personally,' was the disappointed reply.

Culture tip

The Japanese do their homework on a company and its background before any initial contact is made, so the presentation the Brits made was redundant: the Japanese already knew about it. The visitors were there not to negotiate or make decisions, but to determine whether developing the relationship was viable. After that, representatives at the highest level from each business would begin making personal contact before discussing any details. The CEO's lack of interest in travelling to Japan would have undermined any chance of the two companies striking a deal. It is important to understand that an invitation to socialize in Japan should not be put off.

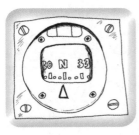

Cultural competence check

To work – or not to work – with strangers.

Relationship-based cultures are cautious about doing business with people they do not know and prefer to have a warm lead, so contact is often indirect. Deal-based cultures are comfortable with doing business with strangers and will often contact them directly, as they are open to do business from the outset.

Study the points below. Put them into two groups: deal or relationship.

1. Maintenance of harmony important, do not like conflict and confrontation.
2. Expect direct, frank, straight-talking communication.
3. Prefer indirect and even vague communication.
4. Rely on close relationships rather than contracts to resolve disagreements.
5. Clarity of understanding important when communicating.
6. Contact potential customers or business partners directly.
7. Get down to business at meetings after a few minutes of general conversation.

8. Rely on written agreements rather than personal relationships.
9. Reluctant to do business with strangers.
10. Have time-bound meetings that start and finish relatively on time.

'How do you contribute to decision-making effectively to those people who are of a culture different from yours? There are big differences out there in how you would present information, and how they would present information to you.'

Confidence booster

When working across cultures never underestimate the importance of time spent on building relationships. You cannot just fly in, do the deal and fly out when engaging with relationship-based people. Ensure you have a solid understanding of the cultural expectations; it is very easy to read things wrongly.

Answers
Deal = 2, 5, 6, 7, 8, 10; Relationship = 1, 3, 4, 9

Creating cultural confidence

Whilst reading this book why not capture your insights and possible action steps as they occur to you? Use the spaces below to record your ideas regarding your relationships with yourself, your team, your clients and your organization.

Your relationship with yourself

Insights   Actions

_____   _____
_____   _____
_____   _____
_____   _____

Your relationship with the team

Insights   Actions

_____   _____
_____   _____
_____   _____
_____   _____

Your relationship with clients

Insights   Actions

_____   _____
_____   _____
_____   _____
_____   _____

Your relationship with the organization

Insights   Actions

_____   _____
_____   _____
_____   _____
_____   _____

Decisions: head or heart

For a German and a Finn, the truth is the truth. In Japan and in Britain, it is all right if it does not rock the boat. In China, there is no absolute truth. In Italy, it is negotiable.

Richard D. Lewis

---

head ... **heart**

Germanic · Nordic · Anglo · France · Israel · Europe · Japan · Far Eastern · Arab · Latin European · Russian · Near Eastern · Brazil · India · Latin America

This instrument compares the degree to which people rationalize decision-making or are swayed by an emotional connection to group concerns: rational or subjective; head or heart.

Culture crash

Lorena Rodriguez, a young Colombian mortgage payment processing clerk, recently started a new job in a bank based in London. She's enjoying her new life, getting used to the way of life in the UK and making great strides in her position. Her boss, the MD Lloyd Jones, is pleased with her progress and with the considerable improvements she has made in her first five months, something that no one else has managed during their initial time in the company.

Early one Monday morning, she receives sad news from home. Lorena tells Mr Jones that her mother has been taken ill and is in hospital. She enquires about taking time off to go home to visit her mother, and is surprised when her boss says she'll have to run it past HR.

Culture tip

In Colombia, as in other South American cultures, hierarchy is prevalent and managers grant requests based on their own personal decisions. Decision making is far more intuitive and instinctual than in many other nations, and so it was natural for Lorena to go straight to her boss rather than the HR department. When Mr Jones informed Lorena that under no circumstances could he allocate time off to her and directed her to the HR office to ask them to review company policy and to suggest options, she thought him uncaring. She was at a loss and wondered what she had done wrong to deserve such treatment. In the London office, policies and procedures had been created so that everyone would be treated similarly.

Cultural insight

Western cultures have developed steps for a rational decision process, which take a type of 'universalistic approach' – they can be used any time and in any circumstances. Simplistically, these include: define the problem, gather and analyze relevant data, consider alternative solutions, identify minimum criteria for success, decide on the best solution and implement the choice. This programmed decision-making process reduces risk and stress for the decision makers as it is a tried and tested formula that everyone uses. Logic prevails.

A decision in these head-oriented cultures has a truth value, which is seen to be a constant. As one manager explains, '...You refer to the architecture rather than to the flesh first; we prefer objectivity rather than emotional attachment.'

Rational head-oriented cultures favour objective knowledge for decision making: 'thinking outside the box' and new knowledge are highly revered, and different opinions are encouraged to provide new insights. Speaking one's mind, honesty and openness are valued. Therefore it is culturally acceptable to ask questions and challenge existing beliefs. Decisions can often be made quickly by an individual who has the authority to speak on behalf of a larger group.

'How you convince someone from another culture is obviously very, very culturally predetermined. You come back here to the question of processing of information; questions of evidence, what constitutes evidence in one culture compared with another culture.'

Culture crash

During our research we interviewed Bob Scott, a senior manager in the oil and gas industry. He said, 'If you are looking at the speed of decision making in South East Asia it's pathetic. They are absolutely hampered by hierarchy. They have to have absolute consensus to make a decision. In the fast-moving, market-driven sector I work in, this makes life very difficult.' This statement begs the question: By what standard and in what context?

Bob continued, 'Everybody agrees that it takes our Asian colleagues forever to make a decision. In the West, we can implement much faster. I find working in Japan very frustrating…'

Culture tip

This example assumes that there is only one process for making decisions: the Western way. This presupposes an acceptance of deadlines as being the ultimate criteria; not so in many countries. Asian, African and South American cultures prefer the process of acknowledging each contributor's status and contribution, all of which take time.

Decision making through logic can be problematic; some cultures find it incredible that logic can be used to force someone to agree or persuade them to another point of view. Objective reasoning, argumentation and sound logic will never persuade. In these cultures, people need to engage with their feelings about relationships and their obligations to others in all walks of life.

'The other thing that drives me nuts is getting the French to make a decision. They will have just one meeting after another, and it goes on and on. Now, curiously, I think the Americans have far more meetings and talk a lot more than the British; when the Americans decide to go, they just go!'

Culture crash

An American IT consultant, Josh Brown, was working with a large electronics corporation in Japan. He had a great idea to improve one of the bestselling devices the company produced. Dying to share his innovative thinking, Josh gathered various influential members of the company together and made a stunning presentation, logically taking everyone through the thinking behind the innovation. He was sure he would win everyone over with his 'no brainer' concept. However, no one enthusiastically supported his idea.

The next day he asked his Japanese friend for advice. 'My dear friend, Josh,' he said, 'have you never heard of *nemawashi*? If you want to get anything to happen in a Japanese business you will have to exercise patience and trust in your colleagues. What you have to do is speak informally with each one and say, "By the way, I wanted to tell you about something I've been working on…" This is the *nemawashi* system. If your *nemawashi* succeeds then your proposal will be accepted for sure; if there are some people who don't like your proposal you can improve it, adding or modifying until everyone is happy. If your idea is bad, it will be cast out before the senior management know.'

'Since Japanese work in groups, the business decision-making process is rather slow. Unlike American businesspeople, who have been authorized to make business decisions within the capacity allowed by upper level management, Japanese businesspeople are not normally given authorization to make a decision alone.'

Culture tip

Nemawashi (*see also* Productivity) is the most important concept you need to know if you want to understand how Japanese companies work; it is the principle of making decisions by consensus through trust at the *wa* level (harmony with nature). The procedure in a European or American company is to arrange a meeting and make a proposal in front of the main team. It is a slick and pretty fast-paced process, with decisions on how to progress being made then and there. In Japan, before making a formal proposal to senior managers you need to make sure your peers agree. This prior informal consultation is called *nemawashi*. To see success, Josh needs to consult his entire department. Once the process of *nemawashi* is complete, the initiating department has permission to make and implement a formal proposal (note this now a group proposal, not Josh's).

In highly group-oriented countries such as Japan and China, you may need to rethink some aspects of your approach to getting a decision. Learn not to expect direct and quick answers to your questions, and allow colleagues to consult each other without being suspicious about it. In such cultures, employees will tend to rely more on the group for support, with aspirations towards orderliness, security and duty. Your reaction may be to view such colleagues as being indecisive and lacking in confidence, while they may be uncomfortable with your demands for individual and rapid responses.

Cultural insight

Consultative authority is the cornerstone of the Arab decision-making process: male leaders at the top, who retain relatively unquestionable authority, make decisions after consultations that range from the appearance of and resemblance to participation. The lower one goes in the hierarchy, the less meaning consultations take and, in most cases, they are non-binding. Consultations seem to be superficial in the sense that the manager seeks to obtain the agreement of organizational members on decisions already made. This projects an image of consultation and participation which reflect the influence of Islam and tribal values and beliefs. The notion of personal relationships is highly valued in the decision-making process, much more than the task itself. Arab executives find that the purpose of consultation is to fulfil the egos of the parties involved rather than to improve the quality of the decision.

Arab managers prefer to rely on their market instincts rather than hard data, so you need to emphasize the short-term effects of the business relationship and/or deal in order to make the proposal convincing and appealing to them.

Cultural insight

Cultures value different types of knowledge. All societies value both explicit and tacit knowledge. However, there is a cultural bias towards one or the other. Data and knowledge are extremely important elements for Western managers for decision making. For them, knowledge is a rational, objective entity. These 'head' cultures tend to prefer explicit knowledge.

In Asian cultures, knowledge and body are as one. There is no mind–body split, as has been developed in Western thinking. Knowledge is not individualized, but readily shared with a network to create a body of knowledge. 'Heart' cultures prefer tacit, intuitive, relationship-based knowledge. Tacit knowledge is highly revered. Remember: people from 'heart' cultures tend to come from relationship-based societies and value group membership as a central aspect of identity, sacrifice for the common good and maintain harmonious relationships with others. Their decisions support those values over logic and speed.

Confidence booster

To influence and persuade people from other cultures you have to win their hearts and minds. It's like the two blades of a pair of scissors: one blade cuts more sharply, but both are needed for the job in hand.

Creating cultural confidence

Whilst reading this book why not capture your insights and possible action steps as they occur to you? Use the spaces below to record your ideas regarding your relationships with yourself, your team, your clients and your organization.

Your relationship with yourself

Insights   Actions

_____   _____
_____   _____
_____   _____
_____   _____

Your relationship with the team

Insights   Actions

_____   _____
_____   _____
_____   _____
_____   _____

Your relationship with clients

Insights   Actions

_____   _____
_____   _____
_____   _____
_____   _____

Your relationship with the organization

Insights   Actions

_____   _____
_____   _____
_____   _____
_____   _____

10 Planning: goal-focused, work–life balance or ad hoc

In the end, it probably comes out roughly square; just a different way of getting there. But in the process of getting there you have all sorts of potential for misunderstanding, breakdown of communications, and breakdown of mergers and acquisitions.

Brian Howe

goal focused	work–life balance	ad hoc

| Anglo | Japan | German | China | Korea | | Nordic | Dutch | Swiss | | Latin European | Brazil | Near Eastern | Far Eastern | Indian | Arab | Latin America | Africa |

How do you undertake a project?

Typically, in Western companies the approach is a goal-based one, where you're thinking about the big picture or your ultimate goal. Goal-centric cultures share the big picture with employees, work with them to set challenging, yet attainable goals, encourage them to be innovative, put systems in place for measuring productivity and give feedback, both formal and real time. This instrument compares the degree to which other cultures follow this 'formulaic' focus on planning.

'The Americans will sell you an idea from a drawing board – they haven't got a product at all. They just get the thing rolling quickly and then try and perfect it as they go … The British will try and make one, and then try and sell it. The Europeans will go for the ultimate specification and seem to take for ever to get there.'

Culture crash

Picture the scene: a global financial institution with a talented, multicultural workforce. The boss tasks Joanne, the team leader and a native Brit, with a piece of work that, whilst important, is not urgent. Joanne creates a workflow chart and schedules Shane, an Australian, with a key task. He responds, 'No worries, I'm good for that. I'm just popping down to the gym first. I'll get on it when I return.' Joanne is taken aback; the German team member is annoyed; the Indian coordinator is mystified. How would you react?

Culture tip

Joanne has the challenge of speaking to Shane to explain the work culture and company expectations of UK organizations. This is work–life balance versus work ethic. Shane can't see what the fuss is about; after all, the work will get done and it was not flagged as urgent.

When you are planning you need to allow for the work styles and preferences of all your team players if you are to maximize their skills and motivation levels.

To Western managers goal setting is commonly regarded as a strategy encouraging autonomy in an individual to take responsibility for a particular outcome. Individuals who are goal focused typically look for the fastest and most efficient way to complete a project. Any consideration that might slow this down can be avoided. Projects can be approached with ease because goal-focused individuals know that they will handle them quickly and efficiently by breaking the project into smaller tasks or steps which can be prioritized, planned and scheduled. These steps give a sense of progress towards the larger goal as they are accomplished one by one.

Culture crash

Anders, a middle-aged Dane, takes up a new position in a recruitment agency in a state-of-the-art high-rise in Singapore. He relocates his young family. At first he feels comfortable in his job, reaches his targets and makes a lot of new friends. He enjoys his evenings walking around Singapore, immersing himself in the fast-paced city.

Anders' targets are then stretched. His manager sets out individual deadlines for the team members. Singaporeans are used to working in a fast-paced working culture with overtime, either at home or in the office. Anders works hard, but being required to work overtime has an effect on the quality of his work.

The manager, although appreciative of his colleague's overtime on various days, comments on Anders' lack of commitment to working overtime every day like his colleagues, and calls for a private meeting with him. To his despair Anders insists that he is allowed to enjoy his evenings, as he does enough work in the hours of 8 a.m. to 5 p.m. Knowing that Anders is a hard worker who has achieved his deadlines with impressive results, the manager finds a compromise.

'…The cliché is the Germans, what I call the Euro-rationals, don't do anything; they don't act unless they understand and plan everything first. Whereas the Brits and the Anglo-Saxons they don't really need to understand to that extent – they will take action long before the French and the Germans. The French and Germans would say, "Yes, but look at all the mistakes, the bad quality that goes in to that".'

Culture tip

Some Western societies are goal focused but only to the degree that it doesn't interfere with work–life balance or a good quality product or service. The Scandinavians, Finns and Dutch preciously guard their weekends for family and leisure pursuits, plan well and stick to deadlines so as not to work overtime. Germans are particularly meticulous planners and the French need to think about all contingencies.

As one international manager explains, 'Americans like to get to market first. Planning for them is about helping them to get things done quickly and then sorting problems out. It's all about "ready, fire, aim". Compare this to the Euro-rationals who like to get things done perfectly first. They go for the ultimate specification. For them it's all about "ready, aim, aim".'

Extreme goal-centrics from individualist cultures, such as the Americans and Brits, see their objectives so clearly in their minds that they can feel, taste, hear, and sense the emotions of their success before they achieve it. The self-satisfaction arising when goals are achieved make these goals an important element of motivation. And this also explains why Americans love planning how to make the American Dream happen. People who are goal oriented appreciate working for an organization where there are opportunities for high earnings, recognition, advancement and challenging work. Goal achievement has priority over quality of life and often takes precedence over family life. Performance and results are stressed. Assertiveness, competitiveness and ambition are virtues. A good manager should be decisive and aggressive.

Story

Michael Hyman, the director of custom manufacturing operations for a medical equipment company, scheduled a meeting with three of his reports, whose interpersonal conflicts with one another were causing his division's strategic objective – to become a global firm – to falter.

Working across India, the United Kingdom and Canada, the three members of his team were summoned to Bangalore to discuss the problems. The Indian director saw significant changes needed and was frustrated at what he perceived as the other two's lack of market orientation and their inability to 'hustle'. He explained, 'There's a bit of a laid-back attitude, especially in the UK. They do not really know how to hustle in a positive way. You need to constantly go back to your customer and explain what you do and what you can offer; be persistent.' In his opinion, the UK and Canada were great at planning and assembling all the pieces to deliver the strategy, but this was absolutely useless if they couldn't 'hustle'. In India, planning was ad hoc and arose from the demands of the customer after successful hustling.

People from more relationship-oriented cultures, such as India, are more ad hoc when it comes to planning. That is not to say they are not competitive or ambitious – modern India certainly is – but the relationships they develop along the way are important. For a goal-oriented person, relationships are just resources for achieving the goal; people who help along the way are useful, but are ultimately not important. For ad hoc cultures this attitude is a travesty. They cannot comprehend such thinking. Why does it all need to be about strategy, the big picture and empowerment, they ask?

Cultural insight

The Japanese and Chinese are very competitive; they plan well and plan for the long term. But it is goal focused *their* way. Good preparation and planning helps them achieve their goals through group consensus and *wa* (harmony). The Japanese have a centuries' old tradition of using a wishing doll, called a Daruma, to help them focus on achieving their goals and dreams.

DARUMA DOLL

The Japanese Daruma dolls come in five colours. Choose your colour based on your goal:

- A red Daruma doll is for luck and good fortune.

- A purple Daruma doll is for health and longevity.

- A yellow Daruma doll is for security and protection.

- A gold Daruma doll is for wealth and prosperity.

- A white Daruma doll is for love and harmony.

The Daruma doll's rounded shape allows it to return to its original position even if knocked over, representing persistence, and is closely linked to a well-known Japanese proverb '*Nana korobi yaoki*', which translates as 'Fall down seven times, get up eight'.

Confidence booster

Creating dedicated time for team members to build cultural language skills pays dividends for all concerned.

Creating cultural confidence

Whilst reading this book why not capture your insights and possible action steps as they occur to you? Use the spaces below to record your ideas regarding your relationships with yourself, your team, your clients and your organization.

Your relationship with yourself

Insights

Actions

_____

_____

_____

_____

Your relationship with the team

Insights

Actions

_____

_____

_____

_____

Your relationship with clients

Insights

Actions

_____

_____

_____

_____

Your relationship with the organization

Insights

Actions

_____

_____

_____

_____

11 Productivity: effective, efficient or empathetic

Research has shown that ... [cultural] values affect ... all forms of organizational behaviour...

Nancy Adler

effective					efficient								empathetic
Anglo	Finns	Danes	Norwegians	Germans	Swedes	French	Far Eastern	Latin European	Indian	Brazilian	Latin American	African	Near Eastern	Arab

PRODUCTIVITY

The dictionary definition of productivity concerns a measure of the efficiency of production: the amount of work achieved in a given unit of time. This assumes an interpretation of the value of time and that a measurable amount of work is the objective – a very Western approach – rather than the satisfaction of passing the time in harmony or without riding roughshod over nature. In our cross-cultural setting, let's revise the meaning to 'how things get done'.

This instrument compares and contrasts three ways to differentiate the way organizations make things happen: effective (outcome driven);

efficient (process driven) or empathetic (people driven). When working across cultures, with a deadline to meet and things not progressing as quickly as you might like, it is worth spending a few moments to consider these differences.

Japan: *Genchi genbutsu* refers to getting your hands dirty – how leaders identify or solve immediate problems. Western managers often mistake this for micro-management: constant and unprincipled interferences with the process. However, these principles are used as tools to shepherd processes and productivity.

Culture crash

The NASA project was well underway with two more years until the launch of the next space station mission. However, undercurrents of tension seemed to be forming between the US and the German teams. Indeed the German team were really starting to resent American interruptions and interference as these were beginning to seriously erode their schedules. 'All these on-track meetings!' exclaimed one German scientist. 'What are they for? We know what we are supposed to be doing, we know when it's got to be done by, we've got the project plan in place, everything is going to schedule – and then we have to stop everything just to have a meeting to see if everything is going to plan. Well, it is!'

Culture tip

Productivity is a result of motivation and what motivates an American does not necessarily motivate a German and it more than likely won't motivate an Arab. The US, the Anglo-Saxon countries and the Finns focus on being effective: they are outcome driven. The 'Euro-rationals' (the Germanic cultures) focus on being efficient, on orderly process. They like *Alles in Ordnung*. You might easily hear a German employee saying something like, 'I am paid to write this code. I do not need to speak to others to write this program.' He is being typically German. He wants to be left alone to get on with the task because he has gone into detailed planning to get to this stage; he likes being efficient, focusing on the 'how' and not the 'what'. The Americans and Brits are so focused on being effective and achieving the outcome that they need to be assured that milestones and deadlines are being achieved; they focus on the 'what' and not the 'how'.

'What happens when you do not adhere to these rules of engagement? You get resisted and blocked. When you're all functional and process driven you'll get a certain reply, of course. But you won't get full cooperation.'

Culture crash

Patrick Gruhn arrives in London to meet with his prospective Kuwaiti clients. Negotiations had been taking place for months. They are at the final stages; it is time to talk serious money and production.

Patrick is somewhat surprised when he finds their meeting is taking place in a hotel lobby and not a private meeting room. He is there to present the project plan, agree the timeline and all the necessary steps for project completion, so undeterred he makes a start. Within moments tea is being served, and then everything stops. One of his clients takes a phone call. Shortly afterwards more people turn up and join in the conversation. They are offered tea. Patrick has no idea whether they are colleagues, friends or family, or all three. Even with all these people around, every now and again, his clients ask him questions that need a confidential answer, one that he is uncomfortable about giving in these circumstances. Ninety minutes after his arrival he still has not had the privacy, seclusion and attention he needs to speak about the project. He has to leave…

Culture tip

It is important to be tolerant in business meetings when dealing with Arab executives. Meetings tend to be considered as social occasions where business parties can talk about other issues as much as they talk about business. Having a focused and a serious business meeting might therefore make the Arab party feel uncomfortable and not encouraged to develop a business relationship. In addition to having flexible agendas, professional business meetings are not private; they are often in public spaces, or the door is left open and there may be many interruptions. Meetings sometimes appear to be social occasions with oblique references to the task at hand. Arabs, Indians, and most Asian and African cultures get things done empathetically. These are people – not task – driven cultures.

Culture crash

The next quarterly meeting of the three-year aid project that the Norwegians were financing in Guatemala was about to take place. This would be the sixth meeting and, in spite of plenty of encouragement from the Norwegians, the Guatemalans had not yet managed to write up any of the meetings' minutes, which had caused the Norwegians to have to write them. Back in Norway, these minutes were an essential part of the process of understanding how the project was progressing, what the next steps were and how the money was being spent; part of monitoring and control needed before the next release of funds. Sigvor, the locally-based Norwegian manager, implored the Guatemalans to write the next set of minutes as she was due to leave the country, and without future minutes the funding would stop. As Sigvor took her place around the table and called the meeting to order, she was astounded to see the minutes of the meeting already typed up and placed in front of her.

Culture tip

It's a wonder that any meeting is ever successful when we realize the variety of expectations that different nations have about their purpose. For Norwegians, a meeting is to account for what has been achieved and agree what needs to be done, by when and by whom. It is run with an agenda that is followed, and people leave with delegated tasks and deadlines that all coincide with an overall project plan (efficient). The minutes are important in documenting this process and the decisions taken. For the Guatemalans, a meeting is about showing continued support and informing others about what decisions have been made informally before the meeting takes place (empathetic). In the culture crash, the Guatemalans have no concept of the purpose of the minutes; even when told they still cannot figure out the Norwegian's logic. Guatemalan planning is ad hoc; subordinates are told what to do and they prefer verbal communication to written ('my word is my bond'), and so do not place much credence in pieces of paper. So, what are minutes for?

'In the US there is a great deal of specialization with experts at all levels. Mexican employees are driven to be flexible rather than specialized. Job descriptions are therefore much vaguer.'

Cultural insight

To understand how things get done in Japanese companies, reflect on *nemawashi*: the principle of informal consensus (see Planning). Once everyone agrees, the physical process of *ringi-sho* begins; the final formal step to getting things done. *Ringi-sho* is an approval document sent to upper management on a new business proposal such as bringing in a new supplier. It goes from the lower to the upper level. If there are five people above the issuer of the *ringi-sho*, all five must read, study and stamp an approval seal on it (the Japanese equivalent to a signature). With all seals obtained, the issuer gets it back and can then begin. This process binds everyone together before anything takes place. The issuer of a *ringi-sho* issues it only when she or he knows that it will be approved by all concerned within the company. The Chinese have a similar system whereby an idea is given 'the chop' – the seal of approval.

Confidence booster

It is mostly in the area of productivity that people throw business solutions at problems that are ultimately cultural issues. The strength of this instrument is that it can break the deadlock and get you into action. Deeper understanding of cultural approaches helps you make course corrections along the way, improving your chances of getting things done as you would wish.

Creating cultural confidence

Whilst reading this book why not capture your insights
and possible action steps as they occur to you? Use
the spaces below to record your ideas regarding your
relationships with yourself, your team, your clients and
your organization.

Your relationship with yourself

Insights   Actions

_____   _____
_____   _____
_____   _____
_____   _____

Your relationship with the team

Insights   Actions

_____   _____
_____   _____
_____   _____
_____   _____

Your relationship with clients

Insights   Actions

_____   _____
_____   _____
_____   _____
_____   _____

Your relationship with the organization

Insights   Actions

_____   _____
_____   _____
_____   _____
_____   _____

12 Rules: rigid or flexible

...In the more developed world, in what I call the rational cultures, there is this huge attempt to make everything standard, to make everything objective.

Brian Howe

---

flexible   rigid

Arab	Africa	Near Eastern	India	Latin America	Far Eastern	Latin European	Anglo	American	Nordic	Germanic	Japan

This instrument compares expectations of how we think people will behave. There are two extremes. One extreme is an obligation to adhere to standards or rules, which are universally agreed by the society in which we live. Rigid, or rule-based behaviour, should apply to everyone whatever their position in society: 'the law is the law'.

The other extreme revolves around our attitude towards our obligations to others.

Judgements focus on the exceptional nature of present circumstances, so rules are situational and flexible (sometimes known as particularist). In these cultures there is an emotional need for rules (even if the rules never seem to work). Statistically, from the comments our international managers made, this instrument was rated to be the second most influential by the overall research.

Every country has its way of saying things. The importance is that which lies behind people's words.

Freya Stark

Culture crash

Sarah Haider, a German, was talking to her English colleague Anne-Marie. Both were young mothers returning to work after maternity leave. They were discussing how to discipline their children. Anne-Marie said, 'I see it as my role to show Ben the rules as a young boy and, of course, as he gets older, how to bend the rules to make them work for him.' Sarah was aghast:. 'You either have rules or you have no rules, but you cannot bend the rules!'

'The real thinking of the Germans is highly structured, whereas the fundamental culture of the Finns is that they come from the wilderness without any rules, any structural thinking.'

Culture tip

The two women realized they would have to learn to adapt to work together as they had some fundamentally different viewpoints.

Rules set boundaries which give us guidelines or limits that identify what we deem reasonable, safe and permissible in people's behaviour. They set our expectations of how we should treat others and how others should treat us, and define our responses if someone steps outside those limits. Such rules are built out of a mix of beliefs, opinions, attitudes, past experiences and social learning.

International businesses think more in a rigid-rules way, looking for standardization. Within this type of Western organization everyone acknowledges the validity of the rules because they bind everyone to a mutual understanding. However, even within the cultures who stick to the rules there are differences in terms of flexibility. The more individualistic and competitive cultures strive to 'get an edge' over others. These people challenge the rules and can be obsessed with doing things their own way while still operating within the boundaries of the rules of conduct. Americans, the Anglo-Saxon cultures and Danes are viewed in this way by most Europeans (think in terms of Britain and the EU!).

There is a chasm of belief and behaviour between north-western Europeans and those in southern Europe, which is one reason why the Germans and Greeks will never see eye-to-eye over the financial crisis in the EU. The most rigid, rules-based cultures are more common in the Protestant cultures of the north because of their religious beliefs around truth as an absolute: good or bad, right or wrong. The Catholic south thinks that God might understand if you have to tell a fib to your friend, so there is more of a 'flexible' approach to the rules. Right or wrong? It depends…

Culture crash

Will Jones, a senior sales manager in a pharmaceutical company working across South America, explained: 'It's like playing football in the fog. You don't know in which direction to go. You don't know where the goal is. You don't know if you're offside. That's until someone shouts!'

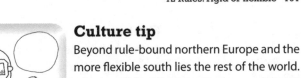

Culture tip

Beyond rule-bound northern Europe and the more flexible south lies the rest of the world. African, Arab, Asian, Far Eastern and South American cultures approach rules flexibly. For them, rules are based on the logic of the heart and human friendship. Organizations in these cultures avoid rigid or standardized systems to manage. Rather, they prefer to leave some room for changes which might occur in the future process. When you put these different approaches together you can have an almighty culture crash, just because the rules of engagement are different.

Culture crash

A few years back, the European Union granted funding to Malawi for a project. Some time later, the Malawi Government applied for more money from the EU for another project. The EU were willing to give more money but they wanted a detailed account of how the previous funding had been spent, as the Malawians had not complied with reporting conditions. Months went by with ping-pong diplomacy and the Malawians still not saying where the money had gone. An impasse ensued. Then the EU decided to grant the African country the funding they requested. They no longer had to account for the 'lost' money but could use it to start the new project. When the project was underway, the EU would release another instalment of funds. Negotiations got nowhere. The project didn't start. The Malawians continually pressed for the money and the EU continually stressed that they should use the funds previously given to them. Soon after, the Danes took over the EU Presidency and all negotiations with Malawi were cut. The Malawians were furious. The Europeans were unyielding.

Culture tip

At the time of the incident, Debby was on an assignment working with the fledgling Malawian Civil Service. Her role was to help bring their communication skills in meetings, negotiations, presenting and reporting up to international standards. One major task was to help them to understand the concepts of accountability and transparency – a challenging task when the group saw nothing wrong with their newly elected President using public funds to restore his personal fortune after spending it on getting elected. They viewed it as 'only fair'. Western concepts of misappropriated funds, bribery and corruption have no currency there.

Culture crash

Kieran O'Brien, a Dubliner and a newly assigned international manager, jets off to Hong Kong. He works as a part of the business development section of The Irish Tea Company, a new and up-market brand in Ireland. He arrives at the office of the leading tea supplier in Hong Kong. He places the contract on the table in front of him with one intention: to get it signed.

The meeting is going great, according to Kieran. Having done research into Chinese business etiquette, he is well aware that he must make his Chinese counterparts trust him and must build rapport with them. At the end of the meeting, the Chinese sign, shake Kieran's hand and the meeting is concluded. Kieran leaves feeling confident and proud.

Several months later, nothing has happened. Repeated emails have gone unanswered. Eventually, the Managing Director, Declan O'Toole, receives an email from their agent in the Chinese office to say that no contract was signed and no deal made.

Culture tip

In Western rigid-rules cultures, a contract formally sets out the obligations of the parties involved. Every detail is written down and penalties are prescribed for non-compliance. Once a contract is signed any flexibility is minimized. Americans, especially, set great store by their contracts and have lawyers on hand to sue over any infringements.

Conversely, in flexible-rules cultures, writing everything down is not regarded as important. A legal contract communicates a starting point for an agreement. As circumstances change so too should the terms of the agreement; the situation and the particular individuals involved are what define the relationship. Strict regulations are offensive and can be viewed as an insult. Contracts are kept vague with room to manoeuvre. People from these cultures prioritize trust and maintaining relationships, so the real negotiations take place long after the talking has begun.

In the culture clash above, Kieran wanted to get the contract signed as soon as possible and has probably already been dismissed in the minds of his hosts. The Chinese signed the contract easily to please their Western counterpart, as they believe details can be changed (or ignored) afterwards. So if you want to do business in China you first need to build a relationship.

Culture crash

Jürgen Schmidt was a senior analyst with a prestige German car manufacturer. During his first visit to Shanghai, in a meeting with a Chinese distributor, he was shocked to see that some of his data and findings had been copied without prior consent. There was no regard to copyright.

Culture tip

Truth and meaning are fluid and circumstantial in China. What we regard as cheating is not perceived as wrong, and designs are abundantly reproduced without permission or deference to the knowledge owner. Knowledge is not seen as a commodity that can be traded, but as an organic element that needs feeding through interaction with people you trust. As knowledge belongs to the community, and not to any one individual, the ethics surrounding knowledge are different from in the West.

Cultural competence check

Behaving 'inclusively' is making sure that you:
A. Know, respect and use similarities and differences in your group to effectively meet your goals
B. Invite everyone to meetings and events
C. Copy everyone on e-mails and correspondence

Confidence booster

What could be regarded as a lie will not be a lie, when there is no bad intention behind it…

Answer

A is the best definition. Knowing and respecting people's differences and similarities will tell you when and where B and C are appropriate and helpful.

Creating cultural confidence

Whilst reading this book why not capture your insights and possible action steps as they occur to you? Use the spaces below to record your ideas regarding your relationships with yourself, your team, your clients and your organization.

Your relationship with yourself

Insights   Actions

_____   _____
_____   _____
_____   _____
_____   _____

Your relationship with the team

Insights   Actions

_____   _____
_____   _____
_____   _____
_____   _____

Your relationship with clients

Insights   Actions

_____   _____
_____   _____
_____   _____
_____   _____

Your relationship with the organization

Insights   Actions

_____   _____
_____   _____
_____   _____
_____   _____

13 Time: deadline or sometime

Danish punctuality would result in hypertension in Greece.

Max Messemer

---

deadline   sometime

| Germanic | Nordic | Anglo | Japan | China | Korea | Brazil | Latin European | Arab | Near Eastern | Far Eastern | Latin America | Africa |

What is time? The value put on time is culturally bound. In Western business, managers want to ensure enough time is allocated to correct actions, which requires a set of skills such as planning, decision making, delegating, scheduling and goal setting. Time is seen as a commodity that, if wasted, will incur penalties along the line. However, different cultures view time in different ways. To some, time is a precious commodity: 'time is money'. To others it's an infinite resource, used to build relationships and watch as God's plan unfolds.

Culture crash

An American HR company hired two foreign interns, a German named Dieter and a Mexican called Silvia. Immediately on arrival they had to work together to support a campaign. They meet for coffee to discuss this new project. 'You're running late!' Dieter said. 'Ah no,' Silvia replied, looking at her watch. 'This is good timing for me, one-ish,' she stated, with a slight pout and shrug of the shoulders. In the end, they decided to come up with ideas individually and meet again to share ideas, agreeing on a Friday 5 p.m. deadline.

Friday comes; it's 5 p.m. and Silvia is late again. Dieter feels resentful. 'Look, I know we were meant to have both parts done by today, but I didn't have the time,' Silvia exclaims. 'My family were over this week. You know how it is.' 'Actually I don't,' Dieter replies. 'We made a commitment to each other. I've done my part even though it was awkward for me this week.' Silvia thinks, and holding onto her cultural roots she smartly replies, 'La hora inglesa, o la hora española?'

Culture tip

There are many different interpretations of being on time. This culture crash demonstrates that Latin Americans are known to turn up thirty minutes late or later. Mexico, for instance, is a 'sometime' culture where time is fluid. Similar cultures are those from South America, Africa, the Middle East and parts of Southern Europe.

Germans are very particular about time; not arriving on time is very disrespectful. You don't waste time in these cultures. Observations around time are task specific; they relate to the completion of tasks with corresponding deadlines. Looking through their task-specific spectacles at nations that are not similarly disciplined, they will always be disappointed. In addition, personal time – interacting with friends and family matters – should be kept out of the office and not impact on work obligations.

Relationship-oriented cultures, ones that take a considerable amount of time to grow close to their partners, view time as an infinite resource, giving people the opportunity to bond with their counterparts. This avoids trouble in the future. If people are not willing to take time now, a relationship is unlikely to survive through ups and downs.

When dealing with clients from different cultures, it is important to understand their view about time, on time or late. Also check out length of meetings, activities such as dinners, drinks and second meetings, as these may be viewed as valuable to your counterparts.

Story

Debby lived in Spain for quite a while and, after a few frustrating months, came to realize that the Spanish word *mañana* didn't literally mean 'tomorrow', but actually meant 'not today'.

Culture crash

Patrick was surprised there hadn't been more changes since the takeover. He had expected that at least a few heads would have rolled, but here they were, all the old senior management team, waiting for a meeting with the new CEO. It seemed the new Indian owners of the British steel works had a real laissez-faire attitude to their take over. Patrick presented his new business plan and spoke about the investment needed over the next five years. He was prepared and ready for questions – except for the two he got: 'Why have you only planned for five years?' and 'What would the plan look like if we doubled the investment?'

Culture tip

Asian cultures have a long-term orientation. Success will come in time with sustained effort. In these organizations, managers are allowed time and resources to make their own contributions. Measures such as market position, sales growth, and customer satisfaction are key in evaluating business performance. These take time to realize and are more important than short-term results. Asians accept deferred gratification of needs. There is an investment in lifelong personal networks and sensitivity to the interrelatedness of social and business contacts.

Culture crash

A group of Irish business people on a trade mission to Hong Kong were about to have an overview of how to do business in China. A meeting with the manager of Enterprise Ireland (EI) had been arranged for 1 p.m. at his office. The group set off in good time to ensure prompt arrival, knowing that the Chinese are particular about time. Due to the hustle and bustle of the large city and unfamiliarity with the transport system, they were still a good half an hour away at 1 p.m. The coordinator received a phone call from the EI manager, wondering where the group was, and saying that he was waiting (somewhat impatiently).

Embarrassed, the group entered the office, greeted by an array of food and drinks – a welcome they were not expecting. Questions and answers followed, and the topic of time arose. In simple terms, the manager told his clients that had EI been potential clients, partners, suppliers, etc, any deal would now be on unstable ground. Out of politeness the Chinese might have waited for them to arrive, or in some cases would have left to tend to other business matters.

Culture tip

The Chinese tend to lengthen meetings, organize follow-up meetings and enjoy entertaining their counterparts with meals outside business hours. They are a group culture, and value time and family time. However, and importantly, when having a meeting with the Chinese it is vital to turn up on time; it is insulting to them if you are late. Other cultures can be a lot more forgiving of 'time wasting'.

Cultural insight

Deadline-driven cultures tend to:	'Sometime' cultures tend to:
do one thing at a time	do many things at once
concentrate on the job	are highly distractible
take time commitments seriously	consider time commitments casually
be committed to the job	are committed to people more than to tasks
show respect for private property; rarely borrow or lend	borrow and lend things often
be accustomed to short-term relationships	tend to build lifetime relationships

Cultural competence check

Under stress, people often revert to the values and behaviours of their earliest upbringing – as well as engage in stereotyping, prejudice and bias towards outsiders. True or false?

Confidence booster

Make time to have lunch with co-workers and colleagues; especially those you don't see regularly. Socialize with people who are important to the success of your project. When travelling to other locations, talk with people you may normally only 'e-meet'.

Answer: True.

We fall back on previously learned behaviours. We call this reverting to magnetic north. All your cultural training may steer and guide you towards the North Pole, but in difficult times our emotions take over. We head for the familiar and comfortable and, as if on autopilot, we end up heading for a safe landing.

Creating cultural confidence

Whilst reading this book why not capture your insights
and possible action steps as they occur to you? Use
the spaces below to record your ideas regarding your
relationships with yourself, your team, your clients and
your organization.

Your relationship with yourself

Insights   Actions

_____   _____
_____   _____
_____   _____
_____   _____

Your relationship with the team

Insights   Actions

_____   _____
_____   _____
_____   _____
_____   _____

Your relationship with clients

Insights   Actions

_____   _____
_____   _____
_____   _____
_____   _____

Your relationship with the organization

Insights   Actions

_____   _____
_____   _____
_____   _____
_____   _____

14 Style: formal or informal

Basic human nature is similar at birth; Different habits make us seem remote.

San Zi Jing

formal   informal

Japan	Far Eastern	Near Eastern	Latin America	India	Brazil	Africa	Germanic	English	Latin European	Anglos	Nordic

Style has nothing to do with right and wrong, your way versus their way. It is simply that people are different and like to do business in a format that makes them feel comfortable.

One of the main causes of failure in cross-border business deals is down to 'inappropriate informality'. This instrument assesses the difference between cultures that are formal and those that are informal. Consider whether the people you are working with prefer a more informal and relaxed style as Britain, Canada, America and Australia – where first names come easily – or if there is a more formal, pyramid structure such as in Japan, China, India and many Arab countries, where people address each other formally, often using titles.

Add to this mix the preferences of the expressive versus reserved communication styles, and you can quickly understand why many deals never reach a happy agreement.

Culture crash

Gregor was a talented Russian IT consultant working in a blue-chip multinational in London. He had very curt, clipped speech and did not engage in small talk. He was regularly late for meetings and often interrupted discussions without taking heed of the agenda or protocol. Jan Brooks, the team lead, felt she had to take Gregor to task.

She met with him on a one-to-one basis in the staff canteen. She offered him a coffee. He declined. She tried to compliment his IT skills and the good work. He stopped her, saying, 'I know what you doing. I know what you are going to say. You think my behaviour is not right and you think it is because I am Russian.'

'Yes,' Jan replied taken aback. 'I was wondering if you would like to take some language or culture classes? The firm will pay for this training.' Before she could explain further, he butted in with 'No!' and almost spat the word back at her. 'My boss tried to help me in Moscow too. But you see I am not just a Russian, I am a bloody rude Russian!' And he walked off.

Cultural insight

Gregor's story makes a good point that sometimes people hide behind their cultural differences; others use them to manipulate situations, circumstances and outcomes to their advantage.

When working in Malawi, Debby was doing research too. She asked people for their 'top tip when meeting a foreigner'. She'd been doing this for many months, in many locations, and received answers such as 'smile', 'firm handshake', 'clear diction' and 'pronounce their name properly'. She asked the civil servants she was working with and to her astonishment they replied, 'Know their status'.

Hierarchical societies tend to be formal. Germans, for example, use lots of titles in the workplace. But societies that have a great distance between those at the top and bottom, such as many African, Middle Eastern, Russian, Asian and some South American cultures, are extremely conscious of status. In asking her clients why they had chosen that particular tip, Debby was told, 'You have to know someone's status before you approach them to know whether you *can* approach them. And then, when you know that, you know what rank you have in relation to them and how you should address them.'

Culture crash

Paulo Ferolota, an Italian, said of a company guest visiting from Texas, 'We took him to a chic restaurant for dinner but he turned up dressed as though he was going to a MacDonald's. He also thought he could tip the waiter with US dollars.'

Culture tip

When it comes to style, the Italians have it. We may think that wearing a tie is formal and an open-necked shirt is casual, but for the Italians dress is important. It is part of the *bella figura* culture about beautiful living and knowing how to live beautifully. There is a code of conduct, a code of dress, and a code of coffee drinking. Their casual manner belies a formal attitude to etiquette. Many of the Latin cultures are similar. In fact, in Brazil, a two-piece suit shows you are just a middle manager, but a three-piece suit shows you are the boss.

Culture crash

Pierre Le Blanc was perplexed and surprised when a new and junior English colleague, John Smith, addressed him 'tu' as opposed to 'vous'. The relationship was put on a bad footing as a result. Yet John thought he was being friendly and doing the right thing by using a little French to show his interest in his unfamiliar Parisian surroundings.

Culture tip

Many languages have different forms for saying 'you'. In French there are just two pronouns: as a general rule, 'tu' is informal and 'vous' is formal. Using the right pronoun to address your counterpart is important in showing the right degree of respect. Some cultures have a different 'you' depending on whether you are addressing a senior male or a senior female, a younger male or younger female and also whether these older or younger males or females are friends or not.

The distinction between familiar and formal speech has almost completely disappeared in English, particularly as spoken by US Americans. This supports the egalitarian American behaviour style – for instance, children often addressing their parents or teachers by their first names. Informality in speech and dress may be seen as a lack of decorum and politeness, or a lack of respect for elders and authority in many cultures.

Cultural insight

Western managers, who tend to be cold and focused on the objective and the details during a negotiation process, should not be surprised if they find that Arab managers tend to be argumentative, aggressive, extrovert and prefer to bargain considerably before signing a business agreement. The negotiating process of an Arab executive is not only different in style, but also in its goal. Arabs prefer to reach a consensus at the end of the negotiating process.

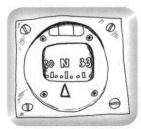

Cultural competence check

Given the effects of globalization and the mobility of people in today's world, you should not expect to find identifiable ethnic or regional cultural characteristics in people you meet and work with. True or False?

Confidence booster

Be ready and flexible for unfamiliar negotiating styles – at the end of the day the success of business deals will depend on your ability to work with different types of people.

Answer: False.

There is a high degree of cultural exchange and fluidity in cultural identity and behaviour, but behaviours that we see are often driven by deeper cultural values consistent with the past. Like detectives, we look for the clues that tell us about these values. This will help us understand, respond and adapt to others appropriately.

Creating cultural confidence

Whilst reading this book why not capture your insights and possible action steps as they occur to you? Use the spaces below to record your ideas regarding your relationships with yourself, your team, your clients and your organization.

Your relationship with yourself

Insights   Actions

_____   _____
_____   _____
_____   _____
_____   _____

Your relationship with the team

Insights   Actions

_____   _____
_____   _____
_____   _____
_____   _____

Your relationship with clients

Insights   Actions

_____   _____
_____   _____
_____   _____
_____   _____

Your relationship with the organization

Insights   Actions

_____   _____
_____   _____
_____   _____
_____   _____

15 Risk: do or don't

One is as many times human as the number of languages one speaks.

Czech proverb

low desire for stability   high desire for stability

China	India	Malaysia	Anglo	Nordic	Germanic	Near Eastern	East and West Africa	India	Latin European	Brazil	Arab	Latin America	Saudi Arabia	Russia	Far Eastern	Japan	Greece

'Do risk' cultures: US, India, Great Britain, Ireland, Sweden, Denmark and Singapore.

'Don't do risk' cultures: Latin America, Latin Europe, Mediterranean countries, Japan and South Korea.

What is risk? Risk is part of every human endeavour. Risk and survival go hand in hand. Risk provides opportunities while exposing us to outcomes that we may not desire. This instrument deals with how tolerant cultures are to risk and ambiguity. On one end of the spectrum there are cultures that are risk taking: open and willing to trying new things. On the other end, there are the cultures that don't do risk: preferring caution, they like to go by the book and prefer to practice tried and tested ways. Risk, therefore, can be seen as the preference of do or don't. To ensure effective business dealings across cultures, you need to understand people's tolerance to risk and ambiguous circumstances.

Culture crash

The vice president of offshoring for a global software company needs a new boss for the team in London. He offers the position to a 35-year-old supervisor, currently based in Tokyo. 'You'll be able to help the team with the guys in the Far East,' he says. After meeting with the current managing director in London to talk about the position, Mr Norisada asks about the structures that are in place at the moment in the London office, and asks what the management team's requirements are for their staff. Is it of a hierarchical nature? Or a level playing field? Do they practice a 'just do it' attitude? 'Absolutely,' replies the MD. On returning to Japan, Mr Norisada decides that he is happier where he is with his comfortably paid job, although a higher position within the company would be nice. He doesn't think he could cope with running the London team: 'It would be like herding a load of cats.' Besides, in not taking this position, his credentials within his company will only increase.

Culture tip

The Japanese are known to be one of the most risk-intolerant cultures on earth. They are renowned for their loyalty to their work, job and career. As in the culture crash above, the Japanese will stick with their job and company hoping to gain a better position. Japanese businesses are very formal (using titles) and structured; decision making is through consensus building, as they are a group-oriented society. The idea of going to London might appeal to Mr Norisada, but he doubts his ability to manage in what is a very individualistic, 'just do it' environment. The loss of his credibility at work, should he fail, would be too much to risk. Besides, he has witnessed the expat 'just do it' approach in Tokyo, and seen it lead to resentment and a lack of support and cooperation from colleagues.

Cultural insight

Business planning in Japan takes account of enormous amounts of detailed analysis of risks. When considering a new business venture, especially with foreigners, there is a deep investigation of facts and figures before making a decision or before any project can start. They shy away from anything unexpected or unpredictable.

Culture crash

The two partners of a high-tech company are looking to recruit a new researcher. One partner is Danish, the other Chilean. There are ten employees at present. The Dane wants to hire a man in his late twenties with a couple of years' experience in their industry. The recruit has an upbeat personality, a very bright entrepreneurial mind, and does not hide the fact he has taken a few risks already in his career which have served him well. Obviously the right sort of guy for the fast-paced and sometimes uncertain environment the industry embraces. The Chilean partner is apprehensive about this new person but eventually agrees to the appointment and ponders on how much he has changed since living in Denmark.

Culture tip

Cultures that have a tolerance for risk taking and ambiguity create organizations that embrace initiative and encourage their employees to take risk, enabling an environment for creativity. The Danish are able to 'do risk': they are innovative, open to change, believe in allowing others to take on projects that are exciting and new. In the culture crash above, the Danish partner wants the new blood and new insights in the business that a young person can bring. A common trait in Danish culture is curiosity; something that has been encouraged and nurtured from a very young age. For Danes, what is different is attractive. On the other hand, Chilean culture is more cautious about risk and has a strong need for structure in the workplace. Chileans tend to rely on and promote existing employees, as they know that they understand the structures in place. They are uncomfortable with change and uncertain or ambiguous situations.

Culture crash

Peter Murrell, the manager of a prestigious bank in London, was both excited and anxious about his next appointment. He had been trying to win the account of an Abu Dhabi-based business for many months. As Peter waited for the chairman and the chief financial officer to arrive he thought how landing this six-thousand-employee company would be quite a coup. Moments later, a young man in his early thirties arrived accompanied by a woman who Peter judged could not have been older than thirty. She was the man's sister.

Culture tip

In the Middle East it is common to see young people in prominent senior positions with large organizations. They have positions of power that have been handed to them by the families that either own or control empires. Whilst expat managers might form part of the senior management team, power and control remain in the hands of the family who hold the director positions. Blood is thicker than water, and when you need someone for an important job, then who better to trust than a member of your family? In the culture crash above, the brother and sister had been given positions by their father; an older sister was chairman of another company; likewise two male cousins. The father managed the group. Many no-risk cultures act similarly.

Cultural compass

How risk relates to culture and organizational structures[*]

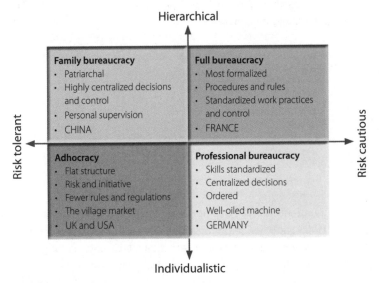

Hierarchical

Family bureaucracy	Full bureaucracy
• Patriarchal	• Most formalized
• Highly centralized decisions and control	• Procedures and rules
• Personal supervision	• Standardized work practices and control
• CHINA	• FRANCE

Risk tolerant ← → Risk cautious

Adhocracy	Professional bureaucracy
• Flat structure	• Skills standardized
• Risk and initiative	• Centralized decisions
• Fewer rules and regulations	• Ordered
• The village market	• Well-oiled machine
• UK and USA	• GERMANY

Individualistic

[*] Based on Hofstede (1987)

Cultural competence check

You are working in an organization where people are used to hierarchical leadership. You want to empower the people who work for and with you. You should:

A. give them vague assignments so that they have to think and exercise creativity

B. make yourself unavailable so they have to make decisions on their own.

C. praise their willingness to follow direction and engage them in more conversations about their work and objectives.

Confidence booster

People are individuals. Not all Germans are process driven; not all Spaniards rely on mañana time; not all Japanese are quiet. Beware of stereotypes. They are useful only in as much as they give an indication of how a person might behave.

Answer

C provides the best starting point of the options given. Both A and B might hinder more than improve individual and team performance. Starting with A might give the impression that you don't know your job and B might send the message that you don't care about them.

Creating cultural confidence

Whilst reading this book why not capture your insights and possible action steps as they occur to you? Use the spaces below to record your ideas regarding your relationships with yourself, your team, your clients and your organization.

Your relationship with yourself

Insights   Actions

_____   _____
_____   _____
_____   _____
_____   _____

Your relationship with the team

Insights   Actions

_____   _____
_____   _____
_____   _____
_____   _____

Your relationship with clients

Insights   Actions

_____   _____
_____   _____
_____   _____
_____   _____

Your relationship with the organization

Insights   Actions

_____   _____
_____   _____
_____   _____
_____   _____

16 Trust: open or closed

People readily ask for help and extend it to those whom they know and trust … Workers find it difficult to adopt practices and suggestions from co-workers with whom they do not have any personal contact.

Transferring Knowledge Across Cultures, **Debby Swallow**

open												closed
US/English/Danes/ Dutch/Norwegians	Anglos	Nordics	Germanic	Latin European	East and West Africa	Near Eastern	Arab	Far Eastern	Japan	India	Brazil	Latin America

There is an unspoken assumption in many global organizations that all those who work for the same company see and react to the world in the same manner, and that therefore trust follows easily. But this isn't necessarily so. There are vast cultural differences that are often not acknowledged or not addressed, and these can create misunderstandings in multicultural teams even before the members have had a chance to meet.

Cultural differences play a key role in the creation of trust, since trust is built in different ways, and means different things around the world.

Research indicates that there are high and low trust cultures; people who are initially open to trust and those who are closed. This instrument compares and contrasts the two approaches.

Guanxi. It's the first word any businessperson learns upon arriving in China. Loosely translated, *guanxi* means 'connections' and, as any China veteran will tell you, it is the key to everything: securing a business license, landing a distribution deal, even finding that coveted colonial villa in Shanghai. Fortunes have been made and lost based on whether the seeker has good or bad *guanxi*, and in most cases a positive outcome has meant knowing the right government official, a trusting relationship nurtured over epic banquets and gallons of XO brandy.

Frederick Balfour

Culture crash

It wasn't a match made in heaven; the Spanish project coordinator and the Russian treasurer seemed to fall out further with each incoming email. One email from the direct speaking, process-driven Russian pronounced: 'The CORRECT version of the sentence from my previous email...' Two emails later and the Russian was asserting: 'I will not write anymore emails to you on this topic. Your tendency to evade answers and misinterpret what I write is unacceptable.'

Finally, the indirect, relationship-oriented Spaniard replied: 'I honestly do not arrive to understand the source of your discomfort, but you can have the assurance that the tone of your last emails is deemed seriously offensive in Spain. I personally do, and I do not accept any more communications in such terms. I resign.'

Culture tip

Written communication is a very real source of misunderstanding, and trust degenerates the more the misunderstanding continues. You can never know what was in someone else's mind when the email was written. Is your counterpart deliberately trying to undermine or insult you?

Pick up the phone and find out. In the story above, the Russian was being pedantic; the detail had to be right; routine and process had to be followed. She didn't intend to offend. However, the Spanish manager found her tone unacceptable: 'She was treating me like a dog and I am a man. I am a man of my word; I can be trusted,' was his explanation.

Generally, Western cultures are more open to trust. However, the US and UK trust more easily than many other European nations, along with Scandinavians, Finns and the Dutch. They generally assume that other people can be trusted until they are let down. Individuals who do not know one another generally assume that they both have positive intentions. Trust is implicitly expected and given at the beginning of a relationship and is reinforced by 'delivering on time' on one's commitments and demonstrating reliability.

Culture crash

An American colleague has lived and worked in fifteen countries, from Europe to the Middle East. Due to constant moving, he is inclined to talk to complete strangers, network and build friendships, all based on a sense of trust. As a result of these short-lived relationships he assumes that the trust he has with each person remains there, and will still be present at their next encounter.

One day he came across an old college friend on his university's website. Happy to be reminded about his Mexican buddy, he linked to him through LinkedIn. After an exchange of emails and a Skype call, our colleague asked his friend to consider becoming partners in a potential business.

However, things did not progress until they eventually met up. 'What I assumed was that we'd just pick up where we left off all those years ago – after all, that's what you do with good friends, isn't it? But with José it wasn't like that. I got the feeling that we were starting over again,' the American remarked.

Culture tip

Creating trusting relationships is by no means a simple process. Unfortunately, as new cross-cultural teams are organized, the issue of trust is rarely considered or addressed explicitly. Taking time to build trust is critical to improving the effectiveness of individual relationships and project teams. Also, as that story shows, never assume that trust remains in place. Trust is 'sustainable' in US, UK and Nordic cultures. As one Finnish manager stated, 'If anything changes, I'll tell you.'

In Germany, trust takes a long while to develop and needs to be nurtured as it will decay overtime, as in Mexico in the case above. The French and Italians are somewhat cynical when it comes to trust. French people who meet by accident in the street are usually on the defensive: each assumes that the intentions of the other are negative until proven otherwise.

All group-orientated cultures are slower to trust; building relationships is a prerequisite for professional interactions. Building trust involves lengthy discussions on non-business topics and shared meals in restaurants. In these countries, getting down to business can only start when your foreign counterpart has become comfortable with who you are. This may take a lot longer than you would consider 'normal'; in the case of Arab and South American countries, it can take months of repeated interactions to establish trust. In the Far East, it can take years.

'People in our part of the world really don't understand networking. They do it but don't understand it. In the Far East ... people want something more professional and strategic from their relationships in the more group-oriented societies. Business is all done on trust.'

Cultural insight

In the Far East you have to be part of a collective entity. In China, *guanxi* (pronounced gwan-shee), the cultural concept of connections and relationships, goes back thousands of years and is based on traditional values of loyalty, accountability and obligation – the notion that if somebody does you a favour, you will be expected to repay it one day. If one person has *guanxi* with another, one will be quick to do a favour, act on another's behalf and, depending on the depth of the relationship, be required to do anything necessary for the other party. In such a way *guanxi* can be considered as a type of currency that can be banked or spent between the two parties. Like money, it is a resource that can also be exhausted, so you must be careful not to become overdrawn. The Chinese are cautious about trusting strangers because they do not know whether you are worthy or not; they fear you may compromise or tarnish their reputation or position. Therefore, they are unlikely to trust you enough to do business with you unless you already have a connection to them through a third party whom they trust. *Guanxi* is often about strategic intent; wanting to know up front what you/they hope to gain from the relationship, to ensure they are not contributing effort or services without gaining something in return.

Culture crash

Gavin Scott, an experienced international negotiator in a UK-based petroleum company, shared his opinion: 'Chinese companies argue, over-promise and bribe. From our perspective, Chinese businesses can be seen amongst the most corrupt in the world. They are more likely to pay a bribe than anyone but their Russian counterparts!'

'Arabs tend to utilize their networks in different aspects of life through what is called *wasta*, the literal translation of which is mediation. *Wasta* is considered as a force in every significant decision. The importance of family connections is so great that when people are admitted to university or hired for a job, *wasta* is more important than their performance in class or on the job!'

Culture tip

Chinese companies are prone to use subcontractors who lack relevant experience since Chinese officials can see this as an opportunity to issue favours. It is not uncommon for officials to renegotiate the original terms of agreements as well, so it is all the more important that cultural training becomes embedded corporate knowledge.

'In China you've got this thing called *guanxi*. *Guanxi* is … a form of you only do business in a circle – in a sort of trust circle – of people you know and have established business or friendly relationships with.'

Cultural insight

Wasta plays a major role in the business negotiation process. Western business people should understand the importance of the networking concept in the Arab world because it has influence in many business activities. For example, negotiating with one company at a time after receiving quotes might be common in the Western world. However, in the Arab world, businessmen can negotiate with several companies and choose the company that they will work with, not based on the contract contents but on the company that had the strongest *wasta* connection.

Confidence booster

When trust is low, perceptions of a problem are distorted. When trust is high, problems are solved. The author Nirmalya Kumar suggests: 'Trust creates a reservoir of goodwill that helps preserve the relationship when, as will inevitably happen, one party engages in an act that its partner considers destructive.'

Creating cultural confidence

Whilst reading this book why not capture your insights
and possible action steps as they occur to you? Use
the spaces below to record your ideas regarding your
relationships with yourself, your team, your clients and
your organization.

Your relationship with yourself

Insights   Actions

_____   _____
_____   _____
_____   _____
_____   _____

Your relationship with the team

Insights   Actions

_____   _____
_____   _____
_____   _____
_____   _____

Your relationship with clients

Insights   Actions

_____   _____
_____   _____
_____   _____
_____   _____

Your relationship with the organization

Insights   Actions

_____   _____
_____   _____
_____   _____
_____   _____

17 Gender: inclusive or differentiated

To understand how any society functions you must understand the relationship between the men and the women.

Angela Davis, author and political activist

---

differentiated   inclusive

Pakistan	Saudi Arabia	Near Eastern	Africa	Arab	India	Far Eastern	Latin America	Latin European	Russia	Anglo	Germanic	Philippines	Nordic

 Iceland, Norway, Sweden, Finland and New Zealand are the five most gender equal cultures; Ireland is sixth; Germany is thirteenth; the UK is fifteenth and the US is nineteenth. France ranks at 46; China, 61; Italy, 74; Japan, 94; Saudi Arabia, 129 and Pakistan, 132.[*]

People from different cultures differ in their beliefs about how justifiable gender inequality is. This instrument compares the degree to which

---

[*] Source: *Global Gender Gap Report 2010*

a society includes or differentiates between the sexes. In addition, societies can be viewed as either masculine (competitive) or feminine (nurturing).

Culture crash

On her first trip to Finland, the British trainer was facilitating some group work when, at 3.50 p.m., Timo got up from his seat, nodded to the trainer and left without a word of explanation. The look of surprise on her face prompted one of the delegates to explain, 'Don't be concerned. It's Timo's turn to pick the children up from school.'

Culture tip

The Finns, Scandinavians and Dutch have the most gender-equal societies. Family responsibilities are shared. Norway requires 40 per cent of its company board members to be women; Finland was one of the first countries to give votes to women. They are also feminine cultures. The social roles for the sexes are relatively overlapping; men need not be ambitious or competitive but may seek things other than material success. In feminine cultures, modesty and relationships are important characteristics.

Culture crash

It was a British-based power supply company and one of the world's leading temporary power-generation rental firms. The new CEO had arrived from the States and, in an effort to overcome some issues arising from working with colleagues in Norway, had invited Debby to give an overview of working effectively with the

Norwegians. On being told that the Norwegians had a very strong work ethic, the CEO replied, 'Not in my view they haven't. They rarely work late and will never put in extra time at weekends.'

Culture tip

Masculine cultures (the US and UK are moderate to high) expect men to be assertive, ambitious and competitive, to strive for material success and to respect whatever is big, strong, and fast; self-enhancement leads to self-esteem. The dominant values in a masculine society are achievement and success. These cultures put in the hours and the overtime. Norway is highly feminine; the dominant values are caring for others and a good work–life balance which is actively protected. Because the Nordic countries safeguard their family and leisure time, this can be misinterpreted by masculine cultures as a lack of work ethic. (See Planning)

Culture crash

An English woman, working for a British motor parts company as a negotiator, lives in the Middle East. She is in a male-dominated industry but her flamboyant nature has served her well in selling into many different countries. Saudi Arabia is added to her patch. During her first visit to Riyadh she is sensitive to decorum, understands the ethics, dress sense and how she is expected to behave. It is important for her to have a male escort, so she takes along her junior male colleague. Imagine her surprise when she undertakes her first meeting and finds herself sitting alone in a room. The clients with whom she is negotiating (all are male) sit in another. Her junior colleague has to run between the rooms to tell the other negotiating party what the developments are and what one party has to say to the other. The role of even the most capable and dynamic senior female negotiator can be challenging in the Middle East. And this was just the first meeting…

Culture tip

The Middle East is very high on the masculine scale. Gender roles are clearly distinct. Saudi Arabia is one of the most differentiated societies in the world, segregating women and men. Women are required to cover up when outside the home and should *always* have a male escort.

A tip for a woman doing business in any masculine country: before you go, find out whether you will be able to meet the client with whom you are conducting business. Unfortunately, you might be seen to be too lowly to interact with the member of the royal family directly. This doesn't only apply to Arab countries but to Asian cultures too.

Culture crash

A successful UK construction company had delivered several building contracts in Dubai. There were many lucrative deals in the pipeline and Greg Martin was confident that he had established a good working relationship with his Arab counterparts. He then employed a marketing director who had little or no experience of working in UAE. It was Christmas time and the new director decided to send gifts of calendars to Dubai. His UK clients loved them, so he did not think to check with the CEO. The response to the prestigious Pirelli calendars was not what he expected…

Culture tip

The Pirelli calendar is famous for its limited availability as it is only given as a corporate gift to a restricted number of important Pirelli customers and celebrity VIPs. The calendar pictures are generally considered 'glamour photography' – naked women. It is a totally inappropriate gift for the region and the reaction from Dubai was immediate shock, horror and dismay. The whole enterprise was jeopardized and Greg Martin had to fly out immediately to placate his client. There was a ceremonial burning of the calendars and a tremendous loss of face. To date Greg has done no further work in the Emirates.

'One Norwegian company has actively decided not to put forward women for potential expatriate manager positions in Japan, as they know that from experience their integration will be difficult. Japanese bosses have a tight network and socialize in a way that does not accommodate women.'

Culture crash

Starting a new job is always daunting; moving to a new country even more so. Else, a middle-aged Danish lady, has made the move to Tokushima, Japan, in order to experience a new culture and progress her career. Before she moved to Japan, she was the general manager in a popular soft-drink company. Else led by example and encouraged her staff to work in an inclusive work environment where each member of the team was treated equally and each role was viewed as just as important as the next. She was more like a mentor than a manager and this put a spring in her step each morning.

On the first day at work in the company in Tokushima, Else was greeted by three well-dressed men: not a woman in sight except for the girl at reception. Instantly she sensed the male-dominated environment and over the next few weeks she began to feel insignificant. Although no one said anything directly to Else, she found her points of view were shunned, her self-esteem bruised, and she felt put down. Her management style was achieving nothing and she was getting nowhere.

Culture tip

In Japan, hierarchy is an all important feature of management. An English male colleague who had been working in the firm for two years explained, 'The work culture in Japan makes a clear differentiation between male and female roles. It is a rigid structure and although multinational companies are more used to women in the workforce, the traditional Japanese companies still only have men as senior managers.'

Cultural insight

A recent survey suggests that: 'Gender inequality causes resentment, anger and reduced life satisfaction more among European and American women than among Chinese women, who value gender equality less. Chinese women consider gender inequality to be less unjust and less unfair.'

Confidence booster

You'll find it best when working with women in masculine societies, such as the Middle East, India and Malaysia, to arrange meetings within their own environments.

Creating cultural confidence

Whilst reading this book why not capture your insights and possible action steps as they occur to you? Use the spaces below to record your ideas regarding your relationships with yourself, your team, your clients and your organization.

Your relationship with yourself

Insights   Actions

_____   _____
_____   _____
_____   _____
_____   _____

Your relationship with the team

Insights   Actions

_____   _____
_____   _____
_____   _____
_____   _____

Your relationship with clients

Insights   Actions

_____   _____
_____   _____
_____   _____
_____   _____

Your relationship with the organization

Insights   Actions

_____   _____
_____   _____
_____   _____
_____   _____

18 Resilience: face or no face

When you travel the world remember understanding is a two-way street.

Deborah Swallow

face										no face
Far Eastern	Arab	Russia	Malaysia	Near Eastern	Brazil	Latin America	Latin Europeans	Germanic	Nordic	Anglo

RESILIENCE

Diplomacy, tact, understanding and sensitivity are all important aspects of resilience because culture can be a fulcrum of conflict from which other issues flow. Conflicts in multicultural settings arise when people talk past or ignore one another or fail to understand nuances. And the nuances surrounding the concept of 'face' are the hardest thing to understand. Bending the truth is common in China and demonstrates sensitivity to feelings; however, pointing out that someone is lying or embellishing will cause them to lose face. This instrument distinguishes between cultures that have a predominantly 'face-saving' approach (from embarrassment) and those who have so much resilience they just bounce back, having 'no face'.

Culture crash

Stan was giving a talk in the Far East on the topic of sales techniques. There was a huge audience waiting for him to speak. His presentation went a lot better than he expected, and so he felt confident enough to ask the audience a question. He continued. 'Has anyone been silly enough to do…' and completed the question. You could hear a pin drop in the auditorium. No one moved. He left the stage confused and wondering what he had said wrong to his audience. He met with a fellow colleague, a Chinese man, and asked him what he could have possibly said to cause such a dramatic silence. His colleague laughed slightly and suggested, 'You have asked them to agree to have done something that may be wrong. If they had agreed and raised their hands they would have lost face.'

The following week Stan again addressed a large auditorium of eager listeners, but at the end he changed the question to 'Has anyone been silly like me…' and continued. The response this time was even more confusing; everyone in the audience put up their hand. Afterwards, he again met his colleague and asked why so many people had agreed. The colleague replied, 'Ah, they all put up their hands so you would not be embarrassed. If you were the only one to have done something silly you would have lost face. They gave you face.'

Culture tip

According to one Chinese social scientist, 'Face is lost when the individual, either through his action or that of people closely related to him, fails to meet essential requirements placed upon him by virtue of the social position he occupies' (Hofstede, 1976). This can be compared with self-respect in individualistic cultures.

Culture crash

A student of our acquaintance was living with a family in China. A couple of weeks into her stay she announced her plans to go into town one evening. The mother told her there was no bus, so she didn't go. A few days later she said she was going into town and she got the same response. When it happened a third time, and she could quite clearly see that there were buses, so she asked a Chinese friend what was going on. She was told this was the mother's way of saying that she didn't want the young woman to go out.

Culture tip

In China and other Asian countries, harmony is very important and should always be maintained. Confrontation should be avoided. It is out of the question to disagree with someone's opinion in public; you would do that in a more private and personal atmosphere to protect a person from loss of face.

In Japan, you have this fundamental concept of *wa* – this basic, semi-religious concept of harmony – between people and *wa*. This means you try hard to work and share through a process of harmony creation

Brian Howe

Culture crash

Gerry Barton, an American lawyer, was visiting Jakarta on business. He hired a car to explore the area and was involved in an accident. Gerry was arrested and taken to the main police station. Although it was soon apparent that he was innocent, the police did not release him immediately. Gerry made a lot of noise and demanded to see embassy officials. When the American attaché arrived, Gerry was released and was told he could not have been released more quickly, otherwise the police would have lost face by admitting they had made a mistake.

Culture tip

People in Western cultures do not get embarrassed or suffer shame as deeply as their Asian colleagues. They bounce back quickly and put mistakes down to experience. Also, Asians have the concept of being responsible but not guilty, and whole boards of directors may resign when a business has bad results. In extreme cases, losing face and being shamed in the eyes of society may mean you undertake an 'honourable suicide'. In the West, people will try and blame someone else, the circumstances, or the economy; the last resort is blaming themselves and actually taking the blame.

'In 'face' cultures, children from an early age are brought up to fear making a mistake, fear bringing dishonour to the family, and fear losing face.'

Culture crash

An Australian engineer has just landed in Tokyo on a week's business trip. He is meeting with one of the top engineering companies in Asia to talk about future business ideas, ideas that will hopefully benefit both countries, and to show them his prototype.

He is met by the company vice president and they head into the office to meet the rest of the team.

The Australian notices that the team seem rather reticent, and not too accepting of his big smile and big handshake. He is handed a business card with two hands, he accepts it and throws his over with a 'here you go'. They assemble together at the lift and to his amusement one member of the team slightly trips; he makes a joke and laughs lightly. Cold silence ensues.

The meeting gets underway. Used to being able to speak up in meetings, the Australian puckers up and questions one of the senior managers, challenges his idea and then places his prototype on the table saying, 'This is what will get round that problem. What do you think of it?' After what seems a long delay, someone asks him when he is planning to return to Australia.

Culture tip

In this culture crash lots of inappropriate and cringe-making actions are taking place. The Australian is seen to be noisy and brash; he jokes about someone tripping up; he hasn't given a small gift on first meeting. He is also unaware of *meishi koukan*, the etiquette surrounding the giving and accepting of business cards – you both receive and give one with both hands. Finally he challenges someone else's idea and then proudly puts his prototype on the table, asking for comments.

Everything the Australian has done so far goes against the concept of promoting harmony. Asking the Japanese to openly critique a new product will not produce the feedback he may want, as any criticism would cause the Australian to lose face. Also, by asking for comments he is not giving face. Instead the Japanese team change the subject – a polite way of saying 'no'.

One of our interviewees, Brian Howe, explains: '...One of the best things to do is actually to give them samples, pass it round the table and let them break into little groups and then they will talk amongst themselves – they will throw it about and look at it, they'll do this – then you'll get a response – but you won't get it by saying, "Come on, what do you think?" or "What are your criticisms?" It is just not in their culture to do that. So these are just simple examples of knowledge transfer.'

Culture crash

Dindra, an Indonesian HR assistant, had been away from her desk for quite a while. The photocopier had jammed again and despite her best efforts she couldn't make the thing work. At this time of day in Jakarta the engineer would take ages to come. So she sought help from a colleague and the two of them were in discussion when Dindra's UK expat manager, Sarah, walked up to them. 'Dindra, look this is how you do it,' she said and then went on to explain and demonstrate further. Dindra, smiling shyly at her boss, remained quiet. Later that day, Dindra told her colleague she thought she would find another job.

Culture tip

In working across cultures trying to transfer knowledge and skills, it is important not only to give respect, but also to allow others to keep their own respect and their respect for you. Face is all pervasive. Giving feedback in Western cultures is normal; we have processes for it, it is done objectively and is not meant as a slight on anyone's character. However, in the culture crash above, the smile from the Indonesian isn't a positive sign. Dindra is embarrassed and feeling a sense of shame, and she feels embarrassed that she has put her boss in this uncomfortable situation. So she 'gives face' to her boss by smiling, thus stopping her boss from feeling awkward.

In individualistic cultures, ideas, knowledge and competence are objective elements that help to form the character of the person, the overall persona, but they do not define him or her. However, for other cultures knowledge and competence are seen to be an integral part of a person's being. An idea or a person's skill can never be separated from the person: these are part of their fabric, their make-up. That is them. To fail in any way brings about dishonour for yourself and for your family. This is why, in group-oriented cultures, group learning and knowledge sharing are so important: they minimize risk of failure and error.

One reason staff suggestions enrich several Asian organizations and participation is so high is because listening rather than declaiming is seen as the more admirable trait. Such cultures do not clash openly. To negate whatever someone else is saying is to ride roughshod over nature. The alternative is to take the proposal on board and alter its import subsequently if it remains unpopular.

Trompenaars and Hampden-Turner

Culture crash

A German engineering consultant in China on a study tour visits an institute where he is asked if would like to give a series of seminars over the next couple of months. Interested, he says, 'I will check with my institution back in Germany to get their approval.' He gets in touch with the institution and receives the clearance, but never hears from the Chinese.

Culture tip

What the German didn't understand was how his need to check was interpreted by the Chinese: he was either a low-status person (because he had to go away to ask a boss) or he was not really interested. Chinese people seldom say 'no' even when it is what they mean. Instead they have numerous polite ways of courteously indicating it. They give face by not giving a rejection.

Culture crash

Abdullah was a construction director on a multibillion-dollar building project in the Middle East. His advisor was a British expat engineer called Joe. An important meeting with government ministers, officials and VIPs loomed. Joe prepared an action plan for Abdullah with methodology, risk assessments and lifting plans. However, Abdullah elected not to take on board Joe's advice. When Abdullah came to make his important presentation in front of his client (the senior officials) it was a disaster (in Joe's eyes). He had not prepared. He bluffed and blundered. What should have been an opportunity to show his skills became a fiasco and a huge loss of face.

Culture tip

Joe felt sorry for Abdullah. He had tried to help him and feared things would not go well, yet his advice had been rejected. Joe had involved third parties and respected senior colleagues, when he realized Abdullah's plans were not sound. However Abdullah refused to listen. Unfortunately, the way Joe gave his advice to Abdullah made him feel as though he was losing face ('I am right and you are wrong'); it left him with no wriggle room. A better way would have been to ask a trusted third party to intervene. To Joe, it seemed that even with the best of intentions and cultural wisdom, personalities and stupidity had overridden common sense and best practice.

Confidence booster

Don't assume everyone is as assertive and open as you. Many people's upbringing requires them to be passive and sensitive, and they will expect you to be sensitive enough to notice if something is wrong. You can't expect them to tell you when something isn't right.

Creating cultural confidence

Whilst reading this book why not capture your insights
and possible action steps as they occur to you? Use
the spaces below to record your ideas regarding your
relationships with yourself, your team, your clients and
your organization.

Your relationship with yourself

Insights   Actions

_____   _____
_____   _____
_____   _____
_____   _____

Your relationship with the team

Insights   Actions

_____   _____
_____   _____
_____   _____
_____   _____

Your relationship with clients

Insights   Actions

_____   _____
_____   _____
_____   _____
_____   _____

Your relationship with the organization

Insights   Actions

_____   _____
_____   _____
_____   _____
_____   _____

19 Quick competence checks

Take people on a well-planned journey… draw out a cultural road map so that if you meet with resistance everyone can see a way forward.

Eilidh Milnes

Assume = ASS + U + ME

There is a popular western mnemonic which says to assume will make an ass (a donkey) out of you and me. Do not assume anything! Get to know people and find out how they view work practices and relationships. Treat your preconceptions only as possibilities, not as facts.

It's as easy as 1, 2, 3.

1. You can't remember 101 different customs for 101 different countries. Start by learning about status, time and style.

2. Ask questions – how do people like to be referred to? How is each person's name pronounced? How do they demonstrate respect?

3. It is not enough to treat everyone the same. Aim to treat people as individuals and as they wish to be treated.

Three communication gems

1. People from direct cultures tend not to accept spoken words as total commitment unless they are confirmed in writing. Follow up telephone conversations with an email or letter.

2. People from indirect cultures tend to regard a written confirmation merely as a simple record and give it no more attention than that. Follow up a letter or email with a phone call.

3. Direct cultures get straight to the point in emails – often without a 'dear XXX' or even a 'hi'. Indirect cultures take time getting to the point. Good practice is always to start with a short greeting and write not much more than can be seen in the preview pane.

Ten tips to ensure meetings run well

Ensure everyone has an opportunity to contribute. Difficulties come when the language of the meeting is not the first language of all contributors.

1. Send out a full, clear and concise agenda to allow everyone time to consider and review the material.

2. Consider the layout of a meeting room. The chairperson should be able to see everyone clearly. If anyone is using a second language during the meeting, put that person close to the chairperson (generally speaking – see 10 below).

3. Americans tend to take up more 'air time' than others, followed by other Anglos.

4. Have regular breaks.

5. Meetings can be tiring. More concentration is needed for non-native speakers.

6. For some cultures meetings are not held for better decision making, but just so that all concerned are seen to be taking part.

7. Set ground rules at the start of a meeting: for instance, time scales, agenda items, meeting format, responsibilities of the people attending, issues of etiquette…

8. Clarify what constitutes a decision and how this will be made. The process of proposing, seconding and voting on an issue moves meetings along quickly but is only culturally congruent with North Americans, north-western Europeans and other Anglo-Saxon cultures. Most other nations look to build consensus and do not welcome being voted out.

9. Consider who will be attending the meeting, their relationships to each other and their relationship to the issues being discussed.

10. People from status-conscious cultures are particular about where they sit in relation to their subordinates and the senior person from the other side, particularly those from the Far East. Do your homework before doing the seating plan.

Ten teleconferencing tips

1. Allow for the impact of time zones. Consult with individuals regarding their preferred time and day for conference calls.

2. Share the burden and rotate time-zone inconvenience if teleconferences happen regularly.

3. Select a quiet space. Be clear on how to use any equipment – practise beforehand – and allow for people joining in and adjusting their settings. Constructively use the 'hello time' as a means to get everyone up and working.

4. Unmuted microphones promote inclusiveness and spontaneity. However, call quality can be poor so mute your microphone when not speaking if appropriate.

5. Keep things short. Attention spans are short on teleconferencing calls.

6. Allow time at the start for social chat. This is seldom a waste of time; it helps bonding and creates trust. Ask people what their expectations are for the meeting.

7. The chairperson needs to be inclusive. People from Asian cultures can be slow to contribute; they are 'reactive' whilst native English speakers seem to dominate.

8. Build in as much interactivity as possible. Use polls to elicit opinions.

9. The chairperson needs to be sensitive to the direct and indirect ways that team members communicate and summarize the points raised to clarify understanding.

10. Be patient.

Ten top tips for better virtual-team working

When forming a new international team establish everyone's preferred working style. Be curious, tolerant and sincere.

1. What are each person's preferred methods of communication (e.g. email, phone)?

2. What is their preferred time for meetings/communications?

3. By what name do they like to be called?

4. Is this about working independently or in a group?

5. Do individuals like to consult with others before making decisions?

6. How will decisions be made: by the team leader, voting or consensus?

7. Share learning from other teams' work, and thus create trust.

8. Build rapport: upload videos and pictures; create a mini website for your team.

9. Team build: write a collective poem or short story. Record a song, silly or serious. Ensure everyone sings a line. Discuss doing something for a global charity.

10. Establish what 'trust' and 'respect' mean to each individual.

Doing better business abroad

1. Learn something about the country, local customs and cultural sensitivities.

2. Err on the side of formality and conservatism. Be low key in dress, manners and behaviour. Very few countries are casual in approach. The Australians are the most casual.

3. Allow time to meet and greet; most cultures need to build a relationship first.

4. Expect your meetings and negotiations to take longer than anticipated. Build much more time into schedules.

5. Politeness and respect matter, especially in the Far East. In many cultures saving face and giving face matter enormously. Avoid being too direct or expecting a 'yes' or 'no' answer.

6. Accents, idioms and business jargon are unhelpful. In Russia and Eastern Europe, for example, business concepts and jargon are new. Check that everyone has understood.

7. Show that you care. Repeat what you have heard in your own way to test you have understood correctly. Actively listening indicates a sincere interest in your colleagues.

Country clusters

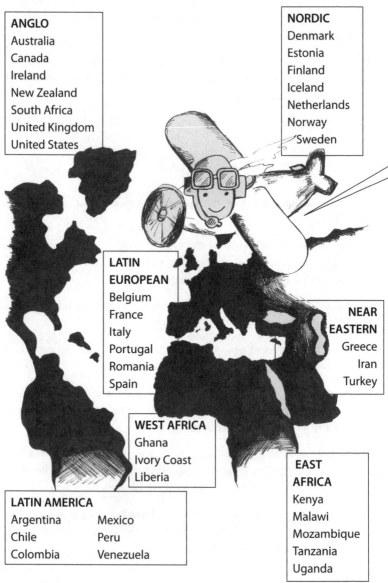

ANGLO
Australia
Canada
Ireland
New Zealand
South Africa
United Kingdom
United States

NORDIC
Denmark
Estonia
Finland
Iceland
Netherlands
Norway
Sweden

LATIN EUROPEAN
Belgium
France
Italy
Portugal
Romania
Spain

NEAR EASTERN
Greece
Iran
Turkey

WEST AFRICA
Ghana
Ivory Coast
Liberia

EAST AFRICA
Kenya
Malawi
Mozambique
Tanzania
Uganda

LATIN AMERICA
Argentina   Mexico
Chile   Peru
Colombia   Venezuela

8. Avoid public criticism or comparison with your own country.

9. Build relationships and trust, which are the keys to successful global partnerships. Only a few cultures focus on 'the business deal'; most of the world focuses on business with those with whom they enjoy a relationship.

10. Learn the customs surrounding gift giving, business entertaining and business cards.

Ten business card tips

Your card is your ambassador – it represents you, so use clean and current ones. Your card leaves an impression of who you are.

1. Exchanging business cards should always be done with respect and decorum, whatever country you are in. It is so easy to make a gaffe. Asian countries attach a lot of importance to a formal exchange while the Brits and Australians do it very informally – like an afterthought. South Africans have no formal exchange protocol, and those from the Middle East or Latin countries are passing you a part of their honour, their 'machismo', with their card. In the Middle East only senior business people exchange them.

2. Always pass your card the right way up so the other person can read it immediately. This shows consideration for them.

3. In Asia, offering and receiving cards is a very formal ceremony: in Japan *meishi koukan* is a very important aspect of business etiquette. Placing the card in front of you on the table is an additional sign of respect. Show respect when you receive a card by using both hands.

4. Always take the time to read someone's card. In our experience, this is special advice for those from Anglo cultures. Other cultures honour the passing of cards. Look at them, study them, and then put them away carefully.

5. Don't put a card into your back pocket; this is disrespectful. Unfortunately, people from Anglo-Saxon cultures have the habit of just taking a card, giving it a cursory glance and (for men) placing it directly into a wallet that goes straight into the back pocket.

6. Don't universally write on other people's business cards. This is a great insult in many countries.

7. The Japanese like photographs on cards.

8. Many US/UK companies are dispensing with job titles, but they are very important in many other cultures. Germans are especially hot on their titles and academic qualifications and expect to be addressed by them.

9. Translate your details on the reverse of the card.

10. Present the card with the other person's language face up. Put it the correct way round for them to be able to read. If it isn't that obvious to you, ensure there is a symbol in a corner that signifies to you which is the right way.

Download our free business card quiz at our website: thediversitydashboard.com/freezone

International negotiations can be a minefield – ten false assumptions

1. International deals will happen automatically if the correct government policies and structures are in place.

2. The successful strategies we use in meetings and negotiating on the domestic scene can apply to international settings.

3. Others' perceptions and stereotyping of us won't be allowed to affect negotiations.

4. Everyone likes to get down to business and focus on the end game: a legally binding contract.

5. A contract, once signed, is non-negotiable.

6. Deliverables will be met according to the contract details.

7. Everyone is after a win–win situation.

8. The 'rules of engagement' are the same all over the world.

9. Decisions are thrashed out around the negotiating table.

10. The use of an interpreter does not necessarily mean that the other person does not speak or understand your language.

Vive la différence!

Every culture is different. Today you need to develop new skills to lead virtual cross-cultural teams to high performance. This will involve understanding all cultural dimensions so that you can generate and formally represent an evolving common culture.

This entails ensuring that communication is clear, coherent and free from intercultural misunderstandings. Your ability to foster successful communication between people of differing cultures will bolster your success in business and in your career.

Confidence booster
Every month pick a language and learn three simple phrases each day for a week – for example, 'hello', 'what's your name?' and 'how are you?' You'll soon have twenty-one useful phrases to build on.

20 Cross-cultural competence

If we cannot end our differences, at least we can make the world safe for diversity.

John F. Kennedy

To be a savvy global traveller you need to develop the skills and mindset that goes with cross-cultural competence. As previously stated, without this intercultural understanding, the MIS Factor is at play: MISperception leading to MISinterpretation, causing MISevaluation that creates MIStrust.

Use the Diversity Dashboard to assess the cultural differences at play in the workplace but also be mindful of the competencies and attributes that enable people to build strong international links and become more effective at working with people from different cultural backgrounds. The competencies below, taken from *The International Profiler*™*, are seen to be the most important.

---

* These competences have been taken from *The International Profiler*™ which is a tool to facilitate international business relationships developed by WorldWork Ltd. The tool helps people working with partners from other cultures to build effective international links. It enables an individual to plan and implement a practical plan to become more effective at working with people from different cultural backgrounds. See www.worldwork.biz. © Copyright WorldWork Ltd. Read more in chapter 3.

Be open

When you pilot yourself across the world, be receptive to new ideas, seek to extend understanding into new fields. As you work more internationally you will be exposed to ideas and approaches with which you may be unfamiliar. Embrace them.

Welcome strangers, be keen and enthusiastic to initiate contact and build relationships with new people, including those who have different experiences, perceptions, and values from yourself. Take a particular interest in strangers. Revel in the unfamiliar and explore differences.

Don't just tolerate but positively accept behaviour that is very different to your own. In an international context, try not to feel threatened or intolerant of working practices that conflict with your own sense of best practice.

Be flexible

Adapt easily to a range of different social and cultural situations, showing a willingness to learn a wider range of behaviour patterns. A readiness to experiment with different behaviours to find the most acceptable and effective ones is a quality worth pursuing.

Flexible judgement will avoid you coming to quick and definitive conclusions about new people and situations you encounter. Use each experience of the people you encounter from a different culture to question your assumptions and modify stereotypes about how such people operate.

People who are eager to learn other languages – even if only at a basic level – show a willingness to collaborate. Being motivated to learn and use specific important business language, over and beyond the lingua franca in which you conduct your everyday business activities, will make a great impression as well as give personal satisfaction. A readiness to draw on key expressions and words from the languages of these international contacts builds trust and shows respect.

Personal autonomy

Holding strong personal values and beliefs, which provide consistency or balance when dealing with unfamiliar circumstances, gives you a sense of purpose when you are faced with pressures which question your judgement or challenge your self-worth. Such values also give importance and credibility to the tasks that you have to perform.

When you set specific goals and tasks in international projects you are more likely to succeed. Combine this with a high degree of persistence in achieving them regardless of pressures to compromise and distractions on the way. People who believe they have a strong element of control over their own destiny can make things happen in the world around them.

Emotional strength

Savvy global workers are usually tough enough to risk making mistakes as a way of learning. They are able to overcome any embarrassment, criticism or negative feedback they may encounter. So be optimistic in your approach to life and develop an ability to bounce back if and when things go wrong (and they do).

Are you able to cope and deal with change and high levels of pressure, even in unfamiliar situations? Can you remain calm under pressure and have well-developed means of coping even when your normal support networks are on the other side of the world? Do you have the personal resources necessary to deal effectively with the stress from culture shock? If so, you have a developing spirit of adventure – you are ready to seek out variety, change and stimulation in life, and avoid safe and predictable environments. As you push yourself into uncomfortable and ambiguous situations, often unsure whether you have the skills required to be successful, you will continue to develop your 'savvy pilot profile'.

Perceptiveness

You need to stay tuned to cultural nuances with your antennae focused to picking up on meaning from indirect signals such as intonation, eye contact and body language. As you become adept at observing these signals and reading them correctly in different contexts, you are almost learning a new language – possibly one of the most important skills you will acquire.

Become more and more conscious of how you come across to others in an intercultural context; be particularly sensitive to how your own 'normal' patterns of communication and behaviour are interpreted in the minds of international partners. This reflection is a powerful exercise.

Listening orientation

Be an active listener. Check and clarify, rather than assume understanding, by paraphrasing and exploring the words that the other people use and the meaning they attach to them.

Transparency

Be conscious of the need for a low-risk style that minimizes the potential for misunderstandings in an international context. Develop the ability to adapt how a message is delivered (rather than just what is said) to be more clearly understood by an international audience. What is required is clarity of communication coupled with the skill to build and maintain trust in an international context by signalling positive intentions, and putting needs into a clear and explicit context.

Cultural knowledge

Take time and have the interest to learn and gather information about unfamiliar cultures, and deepen your understanding of those you already know. Employ various strategies for understanding the specific context they require. At the same time, value and celebrate differences. Appreciate the joy of working with people from diverse backgrounds. Be sensitive to how people see the world differently – not only exploring and understanding others' values and beliefs, but also communicating respect for them.

Influencing

When you exhibit warmth and attentiveness as you build relationships in a variety of contexts, it puts a premium on choosing verbal and non-verbal behaviours that are comfortable for international counterparts, thus building a sense of 'we' and 'us'. This, in the longer term, translates to meeting the criteria for trust required by your new international partners.

Be aware of a wide range of styles. Develop a variety of means for influencing people across a range of international contexts. This will give you a greater capacity to 'lead' an international partner in a style with which he or she feels comfortable.

As you do so, it is wise to be sensitive to context. By that we mean being good at understanding where political power lies in organizations and keen to figure out how best to play to this. Put energy into understanding the different cultural contexts in which messages are sent and decisions are made.

Synergy

And finally, create fresh options. The need for a careful and systematic approach to facilitating group and team work to ensure that different cultural perspectives are not suppressed but are properly understood and used in the problem solving process shows a sensitivity that is not only attractive but is also compelling.

Endnote: coming in to land

There are two ways of learning to ride a fractious horse: one is to get on him and learn by actual practice how each motion and trick may be best met; the other is to sit on a fence and watch the beast a while and then retire to the house and at leisure figure out the best way of overcoming his jumps and kicks. The latter system is the safer, but the former, on the whole, turns out the larger proportion of good riders. It is very much the same thing in learning to ride a flying machine ... The manner in which we have to meet the irregularities of the wind, when soaring in the air, can only be learnt by being in the air itself.

Wilbur Wright

Just as Wilbur Wright advises, being a savvy global traveller can only be learned by 'being in the air itself'. We hope this book has started you on a journey of intercultural discovery. At the beginning you may have thought, 'As long as we all speak the same language, there's no problem,' (stage 1: Denial, see page 25). Reading this book and reflecting on your day-to-day experiences will, we hope, have brought you past thinking that no matter what their culture, people are pretty much motivated by the same things (stage 3: Minimization).

You should now have an easy acceptance of the differences between us and their impact on business performance (stage 4: Acceptance). So, now is the time to take to the skies, experience the turbulences and learn to navigate through them. At stage four you may feel it's confusing, knowing that values are different in various cultures and wanting to be respectful, but still wanting to maintain your own core values. Now you need to build on your enthusiasm for 'difference-seeking' to see more profound contrasts. Seek to develop your communication skills and use empathy effectively to understand and be understood across cultural boundaries, and to journey on to the next stage.

At stage 5 (Adaptation) you feel you can maintain your values and also behave in culturally appropriate ways. You understand that you need to adapt your point of view or behaviour to communicate respect or to solve a dispute. And you can do that without compromising who you are. Seek now to interact with previously unexplored cultural contexts, experience some new 'culture shocks' and evaluate what you have learned. This will help you journey to the final stage (Integration) where you enjoy participating fully in both your own and other cultures and you realize that your own decision-making skills are enhanced by having multiple frames of reference. Now you can truly call yourself a global manager!

Enjoy the journey and travel safely with *The Diversity Dashboard* at your side!

Bibliography and useful links

The authors wish to acknowledge the following as sources for this book:

Bennett, Milton, *Developmental Model of Intercultural Sensitivity* (1994) www.idrinstitute.org

Hall, Edward T, *The Silent Language* (1959)

Hofstede, Geert, *Cultures and Organizations* (1991)

Lewis, Richard D, *When Cultures Collide: leading across cultures* (2006)

Lewis, Richard D, *When Teams Collide* (2012)

Mole, John, *Mind Your Manners: managing business culture in Europe* (1995)

Rosinski, Philippe, *Coaching Across Cultures* (2003)

Schneider, Susan C & Barsoux, J-L, *Managing Across Cultures* (2002)

Simons, George, Diversophy Card Games and resources at http://www.diversophy.com/

Swallow, D J A, *Accounting for Culture in Theories of Knowledge: transferring knowledge and skills across cultures* (2007)

Tomalin, Barry & Nicks, M, *The World's Business Cultures and How to Unlock Them* (2008)

Trompenaars, Fons & Hampden-Turner, C, *Riding The Waves of Culture: understanding cultural diversity in business* (1997)

WorldWork Ltd, The International Profiler plus other tools and resources: http://worldwork.biz/

Useful links

Cross-Cultural Characteristics, http://www.crossculture.com/services/
online-tools (Richard Lewis)

http://geert-hofstede.com/national-culture.html

CIA World Fact Book, https://www.cia.gov/library/publications/the-
world-factbook/rankorder/2172rank.html

World Bank Doing Business, http://www.doingbusiness.org/rankings

Corruption Perceptions Index, http://www.transparency.org/research/
cpi/overview

The Global Gender Gap Index, https://members.weforum.org/pdf/
gendergap/report2010.pdf

Cost of Living Index, http://www.numbeo.com/cost-of-living/
rankings_by_country.jsp

Global Innovation Index, http://www.globalinnovationindex.org/gii/
index.html

UN Human Development Index, http://hdr.undp.org/en/reports/

The Global Prosperity Index, http://www.prosperity.com/default.aspx

The Global Peace Index, http://www.visionofhumanity.org/gpi-data/

OECD Better Life Index, http://www.oecdbetterlifeindex.org/topics/
life-satisfaction/

The Mothers' Index, http://www.savethechildren.org/atf/
cf/%7B9def2ebe-10ae-432c-9bd0-df91d2eba74a%7D/SOWM2011_
INDEX.PDF

WHO Global Health Index, http://www.who.int/gho/publications/en/

Press Freedom Index, http://en.rsf.org/press-freedom-
index-2011-2012,1043.html

Index

Reader resources

This book uses the very latest augmented reality on the cover. Just follow these three easy steps on your smartphone or tablet and see the book come to life:

1. Visit the App Store on your iPhone or iPad, or the Play Store on your Android device, and download the free arpeople app.

2. Activate the app.

3. Use it to scan the cover – to hold the visuals on your device double tap the screen.

Enjoy the little pilot animation. Do let us know what you think of this new technology. Thank you.

To receive our ezine, email **action@thediversitydashboard.com** with 'Free Ezine' in the subject line. This will save you the subscription fee of £60 per year. The ezine delivers tips, exclusive stories and links to popular articles, blogs and multimedia. It will be emailed direct to your inbox every fortnight as our 'thank you' for purchasing this book.

Visit **www.thediversitydashboard.com/freezone** to download a range or resources and support materials.